ROUGH GUIDES

T0085827

POCKET **ROUGH GUIDE**

PORTO

This edition updated by
JOANNA REEVES

CONTENTS

PORTO

Few cityscapes are as remarkable as Porto's. The oldest parts of the city tumble down the steep slopes of the River Douro, a densely packed huddle of tall, pastel-hued houses and church spires connected by a web of narrow streets and stepped alleys. This historic core has UNESCO World Heritage status and has put Porto firmly on the map as a top city-break destination. The metropolitan city area has a population of 1.7 million, making it Portugal's second-largest city; Porto is large enough to warrant extended exploration but manageable enough to be enjoyed over a long weekend.

The *azulejo*-adorned Igreja do Carmo

Barcos rabelos boats on the River Douro

Porto is the oldest city in Portugal and, in fact, gave its name to the country that eventually emerged from the tiny city-state. There's an old Portuguese saying that Porto works while Lisbon plays and, indeed, the city has always been the centre of Portugal's industry. It was here that the ships were built for Portugal's famous navigators who helped open up a maritime empire stretching from Brazil to Macau. However, its most famous industry has long been port wine, a name given by the city but whose production is largely based on the south banks of the River Douro in Vila Nova de Gaia. Technically a separate city, it is closely linked to Porto by a series of impressive bridges and no trip to Porto is complete without a visit to its famous port wine lodges, whose neon signs light up the skyline after dark.

If you're fit enough to tackle its hills, Porto is ripe for exploration on foot: beyond the riverfront lies a fascinating city of broad squares, Neoclassical buildings and Baroque churches, many lavishly decorated with *azulejos*, the beautiful glazed ceramic tiles that also embellish many houses and public buildings. It's easy to get around on public transport, too, with a modern and efficient metro system and a good network of buses. There are also three vintage tram routes, one wending its way along the riverfront to Porto's upmarket seaside suburb of Foz do Douro, whose sands face the roaring waves of the Atlantic.

When to visit

Porto's summers are hot with average daytime temperatures of around 26ºC in July and August. Better times to visit are September and October, which are a more comfortable 21–23ºC, as is June, when you can enjoy the city's main festival, the Festa de São João. However, it's rarely cold in Porto even in midwinter, when it can even feel warm when the sun appears. Be aware, though, that Porto's climate is heavily influenced by the Atlantic and it can rain with a vengeance: the wettest months tend to be October to January.

What's new?

A €100 million complex in Vila Nova de Gaia is reinventing Porto's so-called wine district into a cultural quarter. Opened in 2021, a string of port wine warehouses has been reimagined as a wine school, seven museums and twelve restaurants, bars and cafés. Welcome to the **World of Wine** (WOW; see page 67). Among the highlights are the Chocolate Story, a bean-to-bar overview of chocolate-making; Planet Cork, a fascinating insight into one of Portugal's biggest exports; and the Pink Palace, a temple to rosé with tasting sessions, a giant cask and a Wild West-style saloon. The latest addition is the Atkinson Museum, a contemporary art gallery in a 1760-built house and HQ for port merchant Robert Atkinson.

Porto also boasts some excellent museums, including the seven-strong complex at WOW (see box); Museu Nacional Soares dos Reis, with its amazing collection of art from Portugal and its former colonies; and Fundação Serralves, featuring contemporary art in beautifully landscaped grounds.

The city centre suffered a dramatic loss of population between 1970 and 2010, at which point tourism started to inject new life. Now, many of the previously abandoned or run-down mansions and shops have been reimagined as chic hotels and fashionable restaurants or cafés. Traditional gems remain, too, including the famous Livraria Lello bookshop, allegedly the inspiration for J K Rowling's *Harry Potter* stories.

If you want a break from the city, there are easy escapes out to the sea at Foz do Douro and neighbouring Matosinhos, famed for its fish restaurants, while the metro can whisk you up to Vila do Conde, a historic town with a fabulous Atlantic beach. Alternatively, head inland for a taste of the beautiful interior at Amarante, a quaint town sitting on a tributary of the River Douro, just an hour's bus ride from the city.

Amarante, an enchanting day-trip from Porto

Where to...

Shop

There are plenty of out-of-town mega shopping malls, but the city centre is made up of an appealing jumble of lovely traditional tile-fronted grocery stores, quirky local stores and chic boutiques. The long, pedestrianized Rua da Santa Catarina, near the wonderful Bolhão food market, is the place for everyday clothes shopping, while the area around Praça da Lisboa is where you'll find designer and vintage shops. It's worth heading to Rua das Flores, near São Bento, which is good for chic, independent outlets.

OUR FAVOURITES: Arcádia, see page 54; Fernandes Mattos & Ca, see page 54; Mão Esquerda Vintage, see page 44.

Eat

Porto's cuisine is typical of northern Portugal. Grilled meat – including game and local speciality tripe – dominate menus, as does *bacalhau* (dried salted cod). You'll probably find these humble recipes cooked to perfection in simple, unassuming restaurants dotted round the city, or in the chic (pricier) haunts near the riverside. Don't miss Portugal's famous pastries, either, including the ever-popular *pastéis de nata*.

OUR FAVOURITES: The Yeatman, see page 70; Cantinho do Avillez, see page 56; Piolho d'Ouro, see page 57.

Drink

Porto is forever associated with port, and there are endless possibilities to try it at tasting rooms, restaurants and port wine lodges. There are plenty of other tipples to savour, too, with Portugal's non-fortified wines being of excellent quality. Superbock beer is ubiquitous and there's a growing trend for home-grown craft beers in the city, too. Local brandies are worth sampling, and you should definitely try a caipirinha, a punchy Brazilian cocktail made from a rather drinkable mix of distilled sugar cane, cachaça and lime juice.

OUR FAVOURITES: Café Candelabro, see page 55; BASE, see page 58; Wine Quay Bar, see page 35.

Go out

Porto has a thriving nightlife scene, though note that most clubs don't get going much before midnight. There's a good concentration of fashionable clubs and bars along Rua Galeria de Paris and Rua Cândido dos Reis off Praça de Lisboa, while the streets around the pedestrianized Travessa de Cedofeita are clustered with enticing alternative bars, many of which have nights featuring guest DJs.

OUR FAVOURITES: O Meu Mercedes é Maior que o Teu, see page 35; Plano B, see page 59; Casa da Ló, see page 58.

Porto at a glance

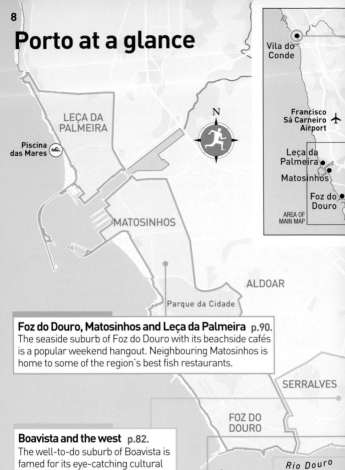

Foz do Douro, Matosinhos and Leça da Palmeira p.90.
The seaside suburb of Foz do Douro with its beachside cafés is a popular weekend hangout. Neighbouring Matosinhos is home to some of the region's best fish restaurants.

Boavista and the west p.82.
The well-to-do suburb of Boavista is famed for its eye-catching cultural centre, the Casa da Música. Further west is the stunning contemporary art museum, Fundação Serralves, with its extensive grounds.

Miragaia and Massarelos p.72.
The attractions of the suburbs of Miragaia and Massatrelos include the Jardim do Palácio Cristal, and the Museu Nacional Soares dos Reis – Porto's top historic art museum.

The Baixa p.48.
This attractive area has some of the city's most historic buildings, best bars and shops, including the famous Livraria Lello.

Vila do Conde p.100.
The easiest escape from Porto, Vila do Conde, is a significant, yet charming, resort home to a long sandy beach, medieval centre and a handsome modern town.

Trofa

Ermesinde

Penafiel
Paredes

Valongo

PORTO
São Cosme

Vila Nova de Gaia

Amarante

Amarante p.106.
The beautiful riverside town of Amarante with its photogenic bridge, main street lined with granite houses and good selection of restaurants and cafés, makes for a perfect day-trip from Porto.

Rio Tâmega

kilometres 10
miles 5

The Sé, Aliados and northern Porto p.36.
Home to a cluster of Porto's most alluring sites including its majestic cathedral, the beautiful São Bento station and the Bolhão market. Further north lies the famous Estádio do Dragão.

RAMALDE

Estádio do Bessa
(Boavista FC)

BOAVISTA

Estádio do Dragão
(FC Porto)

LORDELO DO OURO

CEDOFEITA

SANTO ILDEFONSO

Campana Station

MASSARELOS – BAIXA
MIRAGAIA

BONFIM

São Bento Station

BATALHA

SÃO PEDRO DA AFURADA

VILA NOVA DE GAIA

Ribeira p.26.
Once the heart of Porto's commercial activity, the UNESCO Ribeira district with its waterfront of tall, colourful medieval houses is understandably one of the most popular destinations in the city.

Vila Nova de Gaia p.60.
Tumbling down a steep hillside to the Douro river, Vila Nova de Gaia is the must-visit home of the famous port lodges and the WOW cultural complex. Its riverfront gives stunning views of Porto's historic core opposite.

15

Things not to miss

It's not possible to see everything that Porto has to offer in one trip – and we don't suggest you try. What follows is a selective taste of Porto's highlights, from the city's famous port wine lodges to its coolest night spots.

THINGS NOT TO MISS

< **Port wine lodges**
See page 64
Take a tour and tasting to sample the delicious port at Vila Nova de Gaia's historic wine lodges, some of which date back hundreds of years.

∨ **Torre dos Clérigos**
See page 49
Admire the cityscape from this 75m-high historic tower, a Baroque gem designed by famous Italian architect Nicolau Nasoni in the 1760s.

∧ Boat trip
See page 127
Take a serene boat ride under Porto's six impressive bridges that connect the steep banks of the Douro, each one a remarkable feat of engineering.

∨ Tram to Foz do Douro
See page 91
Hop on the vintage tram to trundle out to Porto's alluring seaside suburb of Foz do Douro, the scenic route hugging the banks of the Douro River.

∧ **Livraria Lello**
See page 52
Check out the decor of this amazing bookshop, whose lavish Art Nouveau interior is said to have provided inspiration for the *Harry Potter* stories.

< **Mercado do Bolhão**
See page 43
Porto's historic central market reopened in 2022 after a mighty renovation – and is even better than before.

< **Casa da Música**
See page 86
Catch a concert at architect
Rem Koolhaas' cultural centre,
a striking chunk of modern
architecture that has revitalized
the Boavista district.

∨ **Fundação Serralves**
See page 87
Visit this stunning contemporary
art museum, designed by
renowned Portuguese architect
Álvaro Siza Vieira and set in
beautiful parkland.

Day one in Porto

Sé. See page 36. Admire Porto's oldest building, then get your bearings from the broad terrace out front.

Walk through Barredo. See page 28. Head downhill through the maze-like steps and narrow alleys of the Barredo district.

Ribeira. See page 26. Explore Porto's riverfront, once rough and ready but now the city's tourist hub.

Funicular dos Guindais. See page 28. Hop on this fun funicular back up to the level of the main city.

Lunch. See page 45. Seek out *Casa Guedes* for its iconic pork sandwiches; nab an outdoor table facing a pretty square.

Ponte de Dom Luís I. See page 40. Make your way over the top tier of the Ponte de Dom Luís bridge for fantastic views across the river.

Teleférico de Gaia. See page 60. You can walk down to Vila Nova de Gaia, but it's more fun to take the cable car which gently glides down to the riverside.

Port wine lodges. See page 64. Tour one of Porto's historic wine lodges, which includes the chance to try the city's most famous drink.

WOW. See page 67. Swing by the World of Wine, a museum complex dedicated to everything from cork to chocolate to, of course, port.

Dinner. See page 32. Walk back over the bridge to Ribeira. Here, you'll find *Adega de São Nicolāu*, an excellent spot for meat, game or fish.

Drink. See page 55. *Café Candelabro* is a great chilled hangout, with a range of drinks in a former bookshop.

The pretty riverside district of Ribeira

Barredo, all pastel facades and tiny alleys

Teleférico de Gaia

Day two in Porto

Palácio da Bolsa. See page 31. Check out the riches that Portugal's merchants once brought to the city at the wonderfully ornate former stock exchange.

Igreja de São Francisco. See page 30. Porto's most fabulous church, a dazzling assembly of gilded carvings contrasting sharply with the eerie catacombs full of scrubbed bones.

Tram ride. See page 73. Hop on one of Porto's vintage trams; the circular route #22 takes you around the city centre.

🍴 **Lunch.** See page 56. There are excellent steaks, *francesinhos* and *petiscos* at the modern *Cervejaria Brasão*.

Torre dos Clérigos. See page 49. Designed by Italian architect Nicolau Nasoni, the top of this distinctive tower offers amazing views across the city.

Livraria Lello. See page 52. You don't have to be a *Harry Potter* fan to appreciate the stunning interior, and exterior, of this historic bookshop, which was the former haunt of JK Rowling.

Fundação Serralves. See page 87. Take the bus to Porto's top cultural attraction, with changing exhibitions in a sumptuous building set in impressive grounds.

🍴 **Dinner.** See page 56. Sample inventive Portuguese food at affordable prices from one of the country's top chefs at *Cantinho do Avillez.*

🍷 **Drink.** See page 58. Chill out at *Casa da Ló,* a former rustic bakery reimagined as a happening drinking den with an inviting little garden and regular live DJ sets at the weekend.

Torre dos Clérigos

Livraria Lello

Porto's vintage trams circle the city

Shopping

There's a wide selection of charming traditional shops, though chic boutiques and mega shopping malls will also keep serious shoppers happy.

Breakfast. See page 44. Start the day in the city's famous and ornate *Café Majestic*, before the crowds take over.

A Pérola do Bolhão. See page 44. Opposite Porto's fabulous Bolhão market, this charming grocery store has barely changed since it opened in 1917 – a must-stop for foodies.

Livraria Lello. See page 54. Even if you don't want to buy a book, this is a must-see magical store that inspired JK Rowling's *Harry Potter*.

Alameda. See page 44. The place to go for some serious shopping, packed with over 120 shops and a giant hypermarket.

Lunch. See page 80. Have an inexpensive lunch in *Rota do Chá*'s Zen-like garden.

Rua Miguel Bombarda. See page 78. This long street is lined by ahead-of-the-curve galleries and cool boutiques showcasing cutting-edge art, fashion and design.

Rua das Flores. See page 48. Meander along this fashionable pedestrianized street, pausing to browse chocolate shops, delis, boutiques and cafés.

Loja de Vinhos do Douro e do Porto. See page 32. Knock back a glass of Porto's famous tipple at the Port Wine Institute's shop and showroom.

Armazén. See page 79. Its name means warehouse, and it's a treasure trove of bric-à-brac, antiques and curios.

Dinner. See page 32. Enjoy modern Portuguese cuisine with a river view at *Bacalhau*.

A Pérola do Bolhão, going strong since 1917

Rota do Chá

Rua das Flores: a chic shopping enclave

Kids' Porto

Portugal is very child-friendly, and Porto has a diverse range of attractions to appeal to all ages, from rattling tram rides to museums and beaches.

Torre dos Clérigos. See page 49. Challenge the kids to climb the two hundred stairs to Porto's best viewing platform at the top of a 75m-high tower.

Douro bridges cruise. See page 127. See Porto from the water on these fun fifty-minute boat trips along the Douro.

World of Discoveries. See page 73. This informative themed museum transports kids back to the time of Portugal's maritime explorations: there's even an indoor boat ride for them to enjoy.

Museu dos Transportes e Comunicações. See page 72. In the amazing former customs house building, this vast museum displays everything from vintage computers to classic cars.

🍴 **Lunch.** See page 34. Try Porto's legendary *francesinhas* at *Verso em Pedra*.

Bazar de Paris. See page 44. Pop into the city's oldest toyshop: it may not be huge, but it certainly has some vintage gems; brace yourself for a dose of nostalgia.

Teleférico de Gaia. See page 60. Take the cable car from Jardim do Morro metro stop (it's a great trip from São Bento metro to get there) for a stunning ride down to Vila Nova de Gaia.

Zoo Santo Inácio. See page 62. A fun zoo where you can walk through a tunnel that takes you up close to Asian lions.

🍴 **Dinner.** See page 47. You can't go wrong with chicken and chips, and *Pedro dos Frangos* specializes in it.

Porto's bridges: best seen on a cruise

World of Discoveries

Zoo Santo Inácio, home to big cats

Budget Porto

Portugal is inexpensive at the best of times but you can save even more by visiting this range of attractions that are completely free to enter, or cheaper than most.

Centro Português de Fotografia.
See page 51. There's free entry to this fascinating photographic museum housed in the eerie former city prison.

Jardim do Palácio de Cristal. See page 76. Relax at these tranquil gardens whose manicured terraces spill down towards the Douro.

🍴 **Lunch.** See page 57. Eat inside the cavernous *Café Piolho d'Ouro* for large portions of wallet-friendly meals.

Cais da Ribeira. See page 26. Porto's riverfront provides constant free entertainment in the form of buskers, street artists, people-watching and river views.

Ponte de Dom Luís I. See page 40. It's a spectacular walk over the two-tiered bridge: the top tier doubles as a metro line.

Mosteiro de Serra de Pilar. See page 61. Admire the view from the terrace of this circular monastery.

Churchill's. See page 65. Take a tour of one of the least expensive port wine lodges and enjoy a free port tasting.

Sé. See page 36. Porto's ancient cathedral is free to enter, while the terrace at the front offers some of the best views over the city.

🍷 **Drink.** See page 47. Make your way to the *Guindalense Futebol Clube* café-bar, which has cheap and cheerful drinks and snacks – plus views to die for.

🍴 **Dinner.** See page 81. Squeeze into the titchy *Taberna Santo António*, where you can feast on bargain daily specials.

Centro Português de Fotografia

Jardim do Palácio de Cristal

Mosteiro de Serra de Pilar

A day by the sea

If you've ticked off the big-hitters, take a break from the city with a day out by the sea at the well-to-do suburb of Foz do Douro or neighbouring Matosinhos.

Tram to Foz do Douro. See page 91. Tram #1 is a wonderful ride out to the sea, following the banks of the River Douro.

Jardim do Passeio Alegre. See page 90. Take a leisurely walk to the seafront via these lush gardens, which are fringed by towering palms and dotted with ponds.

🍴 **Breakfast.** See page 97. Head for *Tavi*, a gem of a café with a sea-facing terrace and a sumptuous array of pastries.

Foz seafront. See page 91. Amble along Foz do Douro's seafront promenade, stopping off at a series of sandy beaches.

Parque da Cidade. See page 94. Take a stroll through Portugal's largest urban park, peppered with lakes, lawns and flowerbeds.

🍴 **Lunch.** See page 98. Hop on a bus up the coast to neighbouring Matosinhos, famed for its fish restaurants – *Dom Peixe* is always a good bet.

Matosinhos market. See page 95. Walk up to the expansive Matosinhos market, filled with an astonishing array of fish of all sizes, as well as fresh fruit, vegetables and flowers.

Piscina das Mares. See page 95. With your own transport, you can head north to these sleek sea pools, designed by Portugal's most famous architect.

🍴 **Dinner.** See page 99. Take the bus back to Foz do Douro for a beachside meal at *Praia da Luz*, a prime chillout spot to watch the sun set.

Jardim do Passeio Alegre

Foz do Douro's seafront promenade

Matosinhos market

PLACES

Igreja de Santo António dos Congregados

Ribeira

Ribeira (which means riverside) is a fascinating hotch-potch of tall, colourful houses piled one behind the other on the steep slopes leading down to the Douro. This was the heart of the medieval city and the hub of its commerce. With the dramatic Ponte de Dom Luís I on one side and the distinctive port wine lodges opposite, it's undeniably attractive, its riverbanks lined with cafés and restaurants that attract no shortage of tourists, buskers and street entertainers. Just back from the river, you'll find some of the city's most historic buildings, including the Casa do Infante, believed to be the former house of Henry the Navigator, the impressive fourteenth-century Igreja de São Francisco, and Porto's former stock exchange, the Bolsa, which gives an insight into the commercial riches that once poured into the city.

Cais da Ribeira

MAP PAGE 28, POCKET MAP E8

The arcaded quayside, the **Cais da Ribeira**, is a highly picturesque run of restaurants and cafés looking across the river Douro to the port wine lodges on the other side. Lined with tall, medieval houses, this used to be the centre for Porto's trade, with *bacalhau*, cotton, wine and other goods being unloaded from the boats that plied the river Douro. Today, the pedestrianized riverfront has become the tourist heart of the city, with places to eat, buskers and hawkers. It can get crowded, but it's still an atmospheric and

Praça da Ribeira, the riverside district's main square

< Palácio da Bolsa
See page 31

The wealth of Porto's nineteenth-century traders is demonstrated by the opulence of the former stock exchange, built in the style of a Neoclassical palace; join a guided tour to see the lavish halls.

> A drink at Ribeira
See page 26

Watch the comings and goings with a glass of white port from the picturesque Douro riverside district of Ribeira, the city's ancient docks.

∨ Ponte de Dom Luís I
See pages 27 and 40

You can walk over the top or bottom tier of this historic bridge. Built by a colleague of Gustav Eiffel, it offers superb views over the Douro.

‹ São Bento
See page 42
You don't have to take a train to admire the stunning tiled interior of the city station, decorated with around 20,000 glazed tiles by painter Jorge Colaço.

⌄ A night out in the Baixa
See page 58
Head down Travessa do Cedofeita or Rua Cândido dos Reis for the liveliest bar and club crawl, though don't expect much action before midnight.

Mind the gap – record-breaking bridges over the Douro

Porto's steep-sided valley has always proved devilishly difficult to traverse. Until 1806, its only crossing was via boats strapped together to form temporary bridges for special occasions. It wasn't until 1843 that the permanent, 170m-span bridge Ponte Pénsil finally crossed the river, and like most of its successors, its span broke world records at the time. In 1877, **Gustave Eiffel** designed the **Ponte Maria Pia** railway bridge, the last major project before he worked on the Eiffel Tower. The Ponte Pénsil was soon replaced by what was then the longest metal arch bridge in the world, the two-tier **Ponte de Dom Luís I**. Designed by Teophile Seyrig, a partner of Eiffel, it opened in 1886 alongside the remaining pillars of the Ponte Pénsil, which you can still see today. There are now six bridges across the Douro in Porto, each a remarkable feat of engineering: in 2003, the **Infante Dom Henrique** bridge at Fontaínhas was opened with the longest concrete arch in the world. The best way to see them all is on one of the many river cruises that depart from either side of the Douro (see page 127).

attractive part of the city – find a perch overlooking the river and you can easily while away an afternoon here.

Towards the Ponte de Dom Luís I, by the arch leading to the Ascensor da Ribeira (see page 28), a plaque known as the *Alminhas* (the souls) marks the spot where local residents lost their lives fleeing Napoleon's troops in 1809. A pontoon bridge collapsed, flinging the people into the river where many drowned.

Praça da Ribeira

MAP PAGE 28, POCKET MAP E8

Café tables spill out onto Ribeira's attractive main square, **Praça da Ribeira**, which is marked by two fountains. One fountain is a modern cube sculpture, known as Cubo da Ribeira, designed in the 1970s by artist José Rodrigues, while the other fountain, Fonte da Rua de São João, dates from the eighteenth century and features a statue of John the Baptist, which the sculptor João Cutileiro added in 2000.

Largo do Terreiro

MAP PAGE 28, POCKET MAP D8

A short way to the west of the Praça de Ribeira, the attractive square **Largo do Terreiro** leads onto a narrow riverfront path lined with cafés and restaurants with riverfront seating. Most of the houses along this stretch have tunnels (now closed) that once allowed produce to be unloaded straight from the ships.

Ponte de Dom Luís I lower tier

MAP PAGE 28, POCKET MAP F8

Porto's iconic double-decker bridge, **Ponte de Dom Luís I**, was designed by a colleague of Gustav Eiffel (see box) and provides one of the city's favourite photo opportunities. You can walk across either level to the port wine lodges, bars and restaurants of Vila Nova de Gaia – traffic runs along the bottom level, while the metro travels across the top level (see page 40). There are steps from the Ribeira up to the lower-level walkway, which lead past a café built on top of the surviving stone piers of an earlier bridge – a great location to stop for a coffee and enjoy an unrivalled view of the bridge and river.

Barredo

Behind the arcades of the Ribeira, the earthy **Barredo** district climbs the hillside towards the cathedral. The best way to explore this warren of alleys that thumbs its nose at the riverside gentrification, is to take the **Ascensor da Ribeira**, a free lift that rises behind the Cais da Ribeira to a rickety platform high above the river. From here, it's an interesting walk back to the riverside: exit the platform at the back (via a few steps) then turn left on the street and you wind down the cobbled lanes. It's about a ten-minute walk back to Ribeira; don't worry if you get lost – that's part of the fun – just keep heading down and you'll hit the riverfront. En route, you'll pass the Torre de Rua de Baixo on the road of the same name, one of the city's oldest surviving tower houses, dating back to the thirteenth century.

Funicular dos Guindais

MAP PAGE 28, POCKET MAP F7
Entrance on Av Gustavo Eiffel
Ⓦ metrodoporto.pt. **Charge.**
First opened in 1891, and closed two years later following an accident, the **Funicular dos Guindais** is a funicular railway running from the riverfront to Praça da Batalha in just a couple of minutes. The cabins used today date from 2004, when the railway was reopened in time for the Euro 2004 football championships. A trip on the funicular makes for a fun approach to the upper town. The route ascends around 60m, and though it's partly through a tunnel, you can enjoy fine views of the river.

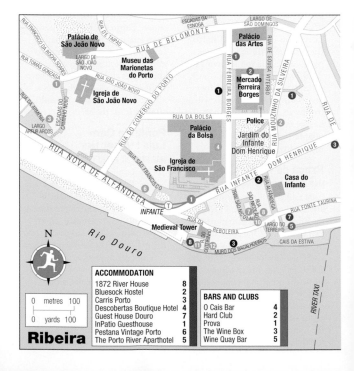

ACCOMMODATION	
1872 River House	8
Bluesock Hostel	2
Carris Porto	3
Descobertas Boutique Hotel	4
Guest House Douro	7
InPatio Guesthouse	1
Pestana Vintage Porto	6
The Porto River Aparthotel	5

BARS AND CLUBS	
O Cais Bar	4
Hard Club	2
Prova	1
The Wine Box	3
Wine Quay Bar	5

Ribeira

Port

Porto is synonymous with port wine, which you can sample in pretty much every restaurant and bar in the city. It comes in either **ruby** (deep red), **tawny** (made from a blend of differently aged wines) or **white** – the first two are drunk at the end of a meal, the last served chilled as an aperitif. The finest red **vintages** are bottled two to three years after harvest and left to mature. A vintage is only declared in certain years, and the wine is only ready to drink at least ten years after bottling. **Late Bottled Vintage (LBV)** is not of vintage quality, but is still good enough to mature in bottles, to which it's transferred after four to six years in the cask. All other ports are blended and kept in the cask for between two and seven years – then bottled and ready to drink. Of these, a **colheita** ("harvest") is a tawny port aged at least seven years in the cask; other fine wines are **superior tawnies**, between ten and forty years old (the average age of the wines in the blend), while **reserve** ports (both tawny and ruby) are decent blended wines.

Casa do Infante

MAP PAGE 28, POCKET MAP D7
Rua da Alfândega 10 ☎ 222 060 400.
Charge for museum; free on Sat & Sun;
exhibitions often free.

Just back from the central riverside stands the **Casa do Infante**, believed to be the house where Prince Henry the Navigator was born in 1394. Built in 1325 as

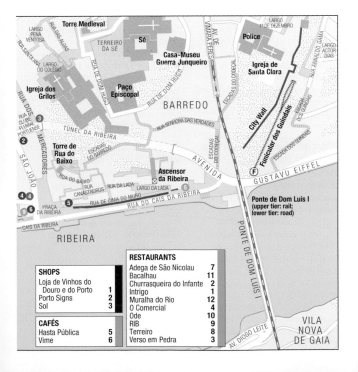

SHOPS
Loja de Vinhos do
  Douro e do Porto 1
Porto Signs 2
Sol 3

CAFÉS
Hasta Pública 5
Vime 6

RESTAURANTS
Adega de São Nicolau 7
Bacalhau 11
Churrasqueira do Infante 2
Intrigo 1
Muralha do Rio 12
O Comercial 4
Ode 10
RIB 9
Terreiro 8
Verso em Pedra 3

Igreja de São Francisco

the Crown's customs house, from 1369 to 1721 it served as part of the Royal Mint. Renovated in the twentieth century, the mansion has been reimagined as a small museum detailing the history of the house, Portugal's maritime discoveries and displaying finds from excavations that revealed the remains of a large Roman palace.

Mercado Ferreira Borges

MAP PAGE 28, POCKET MAP D7
Rua Ferreira Borges ☏ 220 101 186. Free except for special events.

The bright red **Mercado Ferreira Borges** was built in 1885 to replace the old Ribeira market, though the impressive structure didn't function as a market for long and ended up being used as a warehouse. In 2010, the space was given over to the *Hard Club* music venue (see page 35), the *O Mercado* café-restaurant (see page 34) and to operate as a cultural space, but you are free to wander round when events are not

being held here. One of the few buildings in Porto built from cast iron, it is considered of extreme architectural importance and faces the attractive Praça do Infante Dom Henrique, a square gathered round a statue of Henry the Navigator, the Portuguese prince who kick-started the country's maritime empire.

Igreja de São Francisco

MAP PAGE 28, POCKET MAP D7
Rua do Infante Dom Henrique
Ⓦ ordemsaofranciscoporto.pt. Charge.

The city's most impressive and only truly **Gothic church**, the fourteenth-century **Igreja de São Francisco** (now deconsecrated), is even more remarkable for what lies within. The interior had a fabulously opulent Rococo makeover in the eighteenth century, with virtually every surface covered in gilded carvings of cherubs, fruit and animals – allegedly 400 kilos of gold were used to decorate it, at a time when Portugal had become rich partly from the gold reserves in its former colony, Brazil. An impressive granite statue of Saint Francis of Assisi is a rare survivor from the original church. Look out for the church's Gothic rose window and for the Tree of Jesse on the north wall, an eighteenth-century sculpture tracing the genealogy of Christ. The other main feature is the **catacombs**, containing thousands of scrubbed human bones. It's an eerie sight for modern sensibilities, but reflects an earlier willingness to confront, and indeed embrace, mortality before the city had public cemeteries.

Palácio da Bolsa

MAP PAGE 28, POCKET MAP D7
Rua Ferreira Borges, at Praça do Infante
Dom Henrique Ⓦ palaciodabolsa.com.
Charge.

For an indication of the wealth that poured into Porto in the nineteenth century, join a tour of the city's former stock exchange, the **Palácio da Bolsa**, whose interior halls display an almost obscene level of richness. Building started in 1842 to encourage traders to invest in the city's commercial enterprises, on the site of the former cloisters of the Igreja de São Francisco, which had burnt down the previous year. Designed by local architect Joaquim da Costa Lima Júnior in the style of a Neoclassical palace, the lavish interior wasn't completed until 1910, and features contributions from various architects and artists. These include the extraordinary **Salão Árabe** – inspired by the Alhambra in Granada – and the **Pátio das Nações**, the original trading floor, which is embellished with the flags of the nations which traded with Portugal at the time. Note, too, the Sala Dourada, which is lined with the portraits of Portugal's presidents and makes for an interesting contrast to the Sala dos Retratos (Picture Hall) with its portraits of the Braganzan kings who ruled before the birth of the republic in 1910. The Bolsa continued to function as a stock exchange until the 1990s, when it merged with the more influential Lisbon stock exchange. You don't need to buy a ticket to see the dramatic iron, glass and tile Pátio das Nações courtyard, a veritable cloister of commerce, whose side rooms contain a craft and jewellery store, wine bar and shop, and the *O Comercial* restaurant (see page 33). But to delve any deeper into the building, you'll have to bear with the rather pricey and fact-heavy guided visits.

A starter for ten euros

At restaurants, don't feel you're being ripped off when you're served an array of starters before you even order your main course, then get a bill for what you've eaten at the end. This is normal practice in Portugal and no waiter will take offence if you politely decline whatever you're offered. Starters can vary from simple bread, butter and olives to prawns, cheeses and cured meats. If you're tempted, it's a good idea to ask the waiter how much each item costs. Check your bill, too, to ensure you've not been charged for anything you declined. Also, watch out for the **portion sizes**. Many restaurants offer dishes in a *meia dose* (half-portion) or a *dose* (portion) – for most people, a *meia dose* is perfectly adequate and a *dose* is usually enough for two to share.

Shops

Loja de Vinhos do Douro e do Porto

MAP PAGE 28, POCKET MAP D7
Rua Ferreira Borges 27 Ⓦ ivdp.pt.
At the Porto and Douro Wine
Institute's central shop and
showroom, you'll be able to taste a
few wines and then buy from the
well-stocked shelves. It's also a good
place to ask about port wine tours
or to arrange visits to the institute's
labs and tasting chambers.

Porto Signs

MAP PAGE 28, POCKET MAP D7
**Entrances on Rua Alfandega 17 & Rua
Infante Dom Henrique 71** Ⓦ portosigns.pt.
Good for souvenirs and gifts, this
place stocks an interesting array of
handicrafts, including belts, hats
and bags crafted from cork, as well
as ceramics, shirts and toiletries.

Sol

MAP PAGE 28, POCKET MAP D8
Muro dos Bacalhoeiros 125 ☏ 222 083 956.
A fine little cave of a shop that
leads back from the riverfront, Sol
sells pottery, tiles, mugs, plates
and bowls in traditional designs.
There's also an original selection of
attractive fish-themed wall plaques.

Cafés

Hasta Pública

MAP PAGE 28, POCKET MAP F7
Cais de Ribeira 20 ☏ 222 026 001.
A popular café-bar whose tables
have terrific views across the
bridge and river. It serves a range
of inexpensive salads, sandwiches
and pizzas and also makes a fine
stop for a coffee and cake or *pastel
de nata*. €

Vime

MAP PAGE 28, POCKET MAP C7
Rua Nova de Alfandega 12 ☏ 222 010 639.
A pleasant, friendly canteen-style
café down on the waterfront with

large windows framing fine river
views. Good-value breakfasts are
followed up by light lunches of
salads and sandwiches and, later
in the day, heartier evening meals
such as steak or pork and clams.
There are a couple of tables outside
on the street – but watch out for
the trams, which trundle perilously
close. €€€

Restaurants

Adega de São Nicolau

MAP PAGE 28, POCKET MAP D8
Rua S. Nicolau 1 ☏ 222 008 232.
Tucked away down an alley just
off the Largo do Terreiro, this local
place is less touristy than some
of its Ribeira neighbours, with a
cosy dining room opening onto an
outdoor terrace offering excellent
river views. It specializes in good-
quality traditional Portuguese
cuisine, with the emphasis on meat
and game – try hare with beans,
wild boar or half a roast partridge
– though there are also a few fish
dishes. It's small and very popular,
so reserve as far in advance as
possible. €€€

Bacalhau

MAP PAGE 28, POCKET MAP D8
Muro dos Bacalheiros 153 ☏ 960 378 883.
This classy little restaurant has
appealing tables outside on the
river wall – with butter-soft
blankets slung across chairs in
winter – and serves Portuguese
cuisine with a contemporary twist.
Bacalhau, of course, is the main
event, in dishes such as rice with
cod tongue and *choriço*, or turnip
greens with *bacalhau*. There are also
meat dishes, including pork cheek
with bacon and potatoes. €€€

Churrasqueira do Infante

MAP PAGE 28, POCKET MAP D7
Rua de Mouzinho da Silveira 20
☏ 222 000 885.
One of Ribeira's few surviving local
restaurants and a good choice if you

want a change from the touristy places down on the waterfront. It serves large portions of good-value Portuguese cooking, such as grilled tuna steak, veal escalopes or *arroz de marisco*. €€

Intrigo

MAP PAGE 28, POCKET MAP C7
Rua Tomás Gonzaga 90
Ⓦ intrigo.pt.

This restaurant might be tricky to find but it's well worth the search. Expect high glass windows framing Douro views, a simple but classy interior and an enticing outdoor dining terrace. Main courses include duck rice with *choriço*. A better place to enjoy a river view sunset is hard to find. €€€€

Muralha do Rio

MAP PAGE 28, POCKET MAP D8
Muro dos Bacalhoeiros 145–146
☏ 222 423 264.

An unassuming restaurant right on the riverfront, with dining tables outside on the waterfront terrace. It serves a good-value set lunch menu or come in the evening for king prawns drenched in garlicky butter or catch of the day – grilled on the barbecue outside. It sometimes puts on fado (traditional Portuguese music performances) in the summer. €€€

O Comercial

MAP PAGE 28, POCKET MAP D7
Palácio de Bolsa, Rua Ferreira Borges
Ⓦ ocomercial.com.

Grand arches, towering ceilings and racks of wine bottles set the tone for the grandiose restaurant inside the Palácio da Bolsa, the former Porto stock exchange (see page 31). The cuisine offers a modern spin on traditional Portuguese dishes, such as octopus with *migas* (a garlicky bread sauce); scallops and prawns with black linguini or perfectly seared steak with foie gras. Take advantage of the excellent-value set lunch menu (Mon–Fri only) for wallet-friendly prices. €€€

Palatial interiors at *O Comercial*

Mercado Ferreira Borges

Ode

MAP PAGE 28, POCKET MAP D8
Largo do Terreiro 7 ☏ 913 200 010.
Part of the slow food movement,
Ode is small, cosy, stone-clad and
exclusive – the sort of place to
linger. You'll need deep pockets
for this one but the quality is
exceptional, featuring octopus rice,
Iberian pork rib and the sentiment-
laden Grandmother's Pudding, all
paired with the finest Portuguese
wines. €€€€

RIB

MAP PAGE 28, POCKET MAP E8
Praça da Ribeira 1 ☏ 966 273 822.
A smart riverfront restaurant
specializing in meat dishes – if
you're not into steak, it's probably
not for you (the clue's in the name).
While it's not cheap, the food is
certainly worth it. Plus, the bar
serves excellent cocktails. €€€€

Terreiro

MAP PAGE 28, POCKET MAP D8
Largo do Terreiro 11–12 ☏ 222 011 955.
Highly regarded fish restaurant in a
good location with a contemporary
interior and a smattering of tables
on the river-view terrace. The
menu showcases the bounty of the
sea, from lobster rice to *açorda de
marisco* (shellfish bread stew), plus
a variety of simply grilled fresh fish
and seafood sold by weight. €€€€

Verso em Pedra

MAP PAGE 28, POCKET MAP C7
Rua Armenia 12–16 ☏ 222 058 009.
This large, cheap and cheerful
café-restaurant serves the usual
array of grilled meats, fish and
pasta. However, the main reason
to come here is to try its speciality
francesinhas – the seafood version
with salmon and shrimp is
recommended. €€

Bars and clubs

O Cais Bar

MAP PAGE 28, POCKET MAP E7
Rua da Fonte Taurina 2 ☏ 918 397 217.
Steps lead down to this relaxed
bar with a clientele as varied as the
soundtrack. Serves *petiscos*, foreign
beers and mojitos, with frequent

football on the TVs inside. There are also a few outside tables for sun-soaked days.

Hard Club

MAP PAGE 28, POCKET MAP D7
Mercado Ferreira Borges,
Praça do Infante Dom Henrique
Ⓦ facebook.com/HardClubPorto.
In the main hall of the Mercado Ferreira Borges (see page 31), this huge can pack in up to a thousand people. It's a great venue for regular events, exhibitions, club nights and concerts: check the website for what's on.

Prova

MAP PAGE 28, POCKET MAP D7
Rua de Ferreira Borges 86 Ⓦ prova.com.pt.
A dark and dingy jazz bar with a loyal following. Ask friendly owner Diogo for wine recommendations; if he's not about, you can't go wrong with the full-bodied António Madeira red from the Dão region (pair

it with the raw-milk goat's cheese from Beira Baixa for the ultimate in decadence).

The Wine Box

MAP PAGE 28, POCKET MAP E7
Rua dos Mercadores 72
Ⓦ thewineboxporto.com.
Despite its position right next to the entrance of a road tunnel, this fashionable, modern space is a local favourite thanks to its fine range of wines and tapas, such as tuna with pepper, bacon and pineapple and *pica pau* (spicy sausage with a cheesy sauce).

Wine Quay Bar

MAP PAGE 28, POCKET MAP D8
Cais da Estiva 111 Ⓦ winequaybar.com.
Unassuming spot that serves up an excellent selection of Douro wines paired with plates of mountain cheese, cured ham and olives. The best seats in the house are on the waterfront terrace; come at sunset for sublime views over the river.

The Wine Box

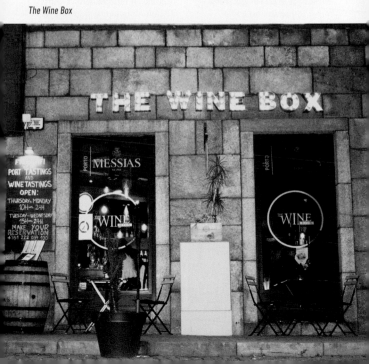

The Sé, Aliados and northern Porto

Some of Porto's oldest and most atmospheric streets are tightly knitted into the steep slopes below the Sé, Porto's ancient cathedral which looms high above the Douro. Here, you'll find the Paço Episcopal, the ornate palace of the bishops of Porto, and nearby, some of Porto's most impressive churches: Igreja de Santa Clara and Igreja de Santo Ildefonso. From below the old city walls the top tier of the Ponte de Dom Luís I offers a dramatic approach to the river's south side, while north of the Sé lie the fabulously tiled São Bento train station, the grand town hall at the top of the main square, Aliados, and the vibrant Bolhão market. North of here, the Estádio do Dragão, the famed home of FC Porto, is the main point of interest.

Sé

MAP PAGE 38, POCKET MAP E6–E7
Terreiro da Sé ⓘ 222 059 028. Charge.

Porto's impressive hulk of a cathedral, the **Sé**, commands the eastern heights above the river. Construction started in the twelfth century and its austere exterior is a reminder that at the time, it was a defiant and resilient structure built not long after the Moorish

Pelourinho da Sé, a 1940s twisted column

occupation of the area and just a few years after Portugal had become an independent country. The building has been greatly enlarged and developed since the original Gothic structure. On the north tower (the one with the bell), look for the very worn bas-relief depicting a fourteenth-century ship – a reminder of Portugal's (and Porto's) maritime past. Despite its great age, there's no real sense of majesty inside the cathedral, with the altar and chapels making little impact in the darkness. The **cloisters**, however, are a different matter, their arched walls filled with magnificent Baroque *azulejos* designed by Valentim de Almeida in around 1730. Italian architect Nicolau Nasoni (see page 49), the designer of many of Porto's grand eighteenth-century buildings, added an impressive granite staircase, which climbs from the cloisters to the restored **Sala Capitular** (Chapter Room), with more *azulejos*, painted ceiling panels and views from the shuttered windows. In the **Tesouro**

The Linha do Douro

Trains depart daily from São Bento station (full timetable on Ⓦcp.pt) along the **Linha do Douro**. One of the most beautiful rail routes in Europe, the Linha do Douro follows the banks of the Douro river valley right into the heart of the dramatic terraces of the port wine-growing estates. A true engineering marvel when it opened in 1887, the Linha do Douro still thrills passengers today. In its heyday, it crossed the border to Spain (for a through service to Salamanca and Madrid) and sprouted some stunning valley branch lines, but even though these branches are no more, it's a fantastic ride – 160km of river-hugging track from Porto to Pocinho, via more than 20 tunnels, 30 bridges and 34 stations. You can take the train all the way to Peso da Régua (just "Régua" on timetables), which is a manageable day-trip, at around two hours from Porto. However, **Régua** also marks the point at which the Douro Line turns from a good route into a great one, sticking closely to the river from then on, clinging to the precipitous rocks as the river – and track – passes through the Douro gorge. Some of the stations are no more than a shelter on a platform, used by the local wine *quintas*, though there are useful stops at **Pinhão** (a pretty port-producing town), **Tua** (a cruise halt with a good restaurant) and, finally, the relatively dinky and nondescript **Pocinho** (around three and a half hours' journey time, making a long day-trip just about feasible).

(Treasury), meanwhile, is the usual boggling array of silver and gold – beautifully lit for once.

Paço Episcopal

MAP PAGE 38, POCKET MAP E7
Terreiro da Sé ⓸ 910 440 044. Charge.

To the south side of the Sé stretches the grandiose frontage of the **Paço Episcopal**, the archbishop's palace. The bishops of Porto first took up residence here in the thirteenth century, and it was here that the first king of Portugal was crowned (and spent his wedding night) – only a small window by the main entrance survives from this time. Most of today's structure dates to the eighteenth century when it was largely rebuilt by Nicolau Nasoni (see page 49), and gives an idea of the bishops' luxurious lifestyle. Construction started in 1772, but took nearly 100 years. Initially, the bishop didn't approve of Nasoni's design; later, in the 1830s, the palace was badly damaged during

the Portuguese civil war and it wasn't until 1871 that it was finally completed. The result is a mishmash of architectural elements: a Rococo stairway lined with carved granite flowers, Neoclassical doorways and Baroque decorations. The tour takes you around all but the bishop's private quarters, the rooms filled with priceless furniture (such as seventeenth-century Indo-Portuguese cabinets) and works of art, including portraits of all the Bishops of Portugal. The palace served as a town hall from the birth of the republic in 1911 to 1956, when the archbishop moved back in – ironically, most of the religious paintings date from this era.

Casa-Museu Guerra Junqueiro

MAP PAGE 38, POCKET MAP E6–F7
Rua de Dom Hugo 32
⓸ 222 003 689. Charge.

With its entrance behind Porto's cathedral, the **Casa-Museu**

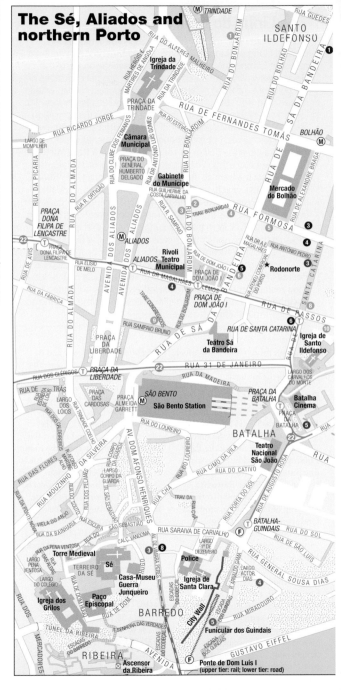

The Sé, Aliados and northern Porto

1 (150m) & **2** (500m)

Estádio do Dragão ▶ **1** (1.9km) & **2** (2.1km)

ACCOMMODATION
América	1
Castelo de Santa Catarina	2
Grande Hotel do Porto	3
NH Collection	5
Pestana Palácio do Freixo	6
Rivoli Cinema Hostel	4

SHOPS
Alameda	2
A Pérola do Bolhão	4
Bazar Paris	5
Casa da Guitarra	8
Comer e Chorar Por Mais	3
Costa Nova	1
FNAC	6
Mão Esquerda Vintage	7

RESTAURANTS
Almeja	4
Antunes	1
Conga	2
Escondidinho	10
Euskalduna Studio	7
Flor dos Congregados	9
Palmeira	6
Pedro dos Frangos	3

CAFÉS
Café Majestic	8
Casa Guedes	12
Combi Coffee Roasters	11
Confeitaria do Bolhão	5
Dama Pé de Cabra	13

BARS & LIVE MUSIC VENUES
Coliseu do Porto	1
Guindalense Futebol Clube	5
Hot Five	4
Maus Hábitos	2
Porto Fado	3

CAMPO 24 DE AGOSTO

Capela das Almas

Coliseu do Porto

Garagem ★ Atlântico

Jardim de Marquês de Oliveira

Jardim das Fontaínhas

N

Rio Douro

6 (2.7cm) ▶

0	metres	200
0	yards	200

Guerra Junqueiro is the Baroque eighteenth-century mansion where the poet, writer and politician Abílio Manuel Guerra Junqueiro (1850–1923) used to live and write his famous works, which reflected the revolutionary turmoil of the Republican era. He spent his lifetime collecting Iberian and Islamic art, and the rooms here recapture the atmosphere of the era with displays of ceramics, glassware, glazed earthenware, jewellery and textiles. The mansion, which was built to a design attributed to Nasoni, also hosts an active calendar of events, including fado performances and poetry readings.

Terreiro da Sé

MAP PAGE 38, POCKET MAP E7

The broad **Terreiro da Sé** is one of Porto's largest squares and the view from the terrace is superb, looking down over old-town streets tumbling down towards the Douro. Although it's surrounded by ancient buildings, the square was in fact laid out in the 1940s when the Estado Novo (the regime under the dictator Salazar) decided to clear away some of the medieval buildings to create a public space. In the square, there's

Ponte de Dom Luís I top tier

the distinctive Pelourinho da Sé, an ornately twisted column which was also placed here in the 1940s, though based on a design dating back to 1797. Just below the square you'll see a medieval tower house, now home to a small tourist office (see page 127). The tower was reconstructed in the 1940s and features a Gothic balcony. Continue downhill from here and you'll pass through the knot of streets, steps and alleys that makes up the Barredo district (see page 28), where locals live cheek-by-jowl as they have done for centuries.

Ponte de Dom Luís I top tier

MAP PAGE 38, POCKET MAP F8

To the east of the Sé, Avenida de Vimara Peres leads down to the top tier of the spectacular **Ponte de Dom Luís I** (see page 27 for the bottom tier). Originally built for cars and buses, the top tier is now used by the Porto metro (take the Santo Ovídio line and this section is between the stops of São Bento and Jardim do Morro), and you can also walk across it for stunning views over the town and the Douro. Continue over the bridge for easy access to the monastery of Serra do Pilar in Vila Nova de Gaia, or the port wine lodges via the cable car.

Igreja de Santa Clara

MAP PAGE 38, POCKET MAP F7

Largo Primeiro Dezembro

ⓘ 223 392 330. Free.

Dating back to the fifteenth century and with a distinctive Renaissance portal, the **Igreja de Santa Clara** was rebuilt in the eighteenth century. Entered through a courtyard, the interior is a glittering magpie's den of ornate gilded wood. After a €2.5 million restoration project, the dazzling marvel has been returned to its former glory and reopened to the public. The Porto School of Wood Carvers spent a whopping five years buffing and polishing the faded

Porto's azulejos

Porto has some of Portugal's best **azulejos** – decorative ceramic tiles – and you can see a variety of styles decorating houses, shops, monuments and churches all over the city. The craft was brought over by the Moors in the eighth century. Portuguese *azulejos* developed their own style around the mid-sixteenth century when a new Italian technique enabled images to be painted directly onto the clay, thanks to a tin oxide coating which prevented running.

Wealthy Portuguese began to commission large *azulejo* panels displaying battles and fantastic images influenced by Vasco da Gama's voyages to the East. The early eighteenth century saw highly trained artists producing elaborate multicoloured **ceramic mosaics**, often with Rococo or Baroque themes as in the interior of the Sé (see page 36). After the Great Earthquake, more prosaic tiled facades, often with **Neoclassical designs**, were considered good insulation devices, as well as protecting buildings from rain and fire. After the mid-nineteenth century, *azulejos* were being mass-produced to decorate shops and religious buildings, such as the fantastic exterior of the Igreja do Carmo (see page 51). By the 1900s, Portugal had become the world's leading producer of *azulejos*, with Art Deco designs taking hold in the 1920s – witness the facade of the Pérola do Bolhão shop (see page 44). São Bento station's entrance hall (see page 42) represents a coming together of all the best that *azulejos* have to offer, a panoply of panels designed in the 1930s by Jorge Calaço representing key scenes in the country's development. Also worth seeking out is the Capela das Almas (see page 43), whose images depicting the lives of the saints are an early twentieth-century recreation of eighteenth-century designs.

gold leaf that cloaks almost every surface of the walls and ceiling. A grill separates the church from an adjacent convent, which is now used by the police.

Igreja de Santo Ildefonso

MAP PAGE 38, POCKET MAP G5
Praça da Batalha ☏ 222 004 366. Free.
Another impressive church is the **Igreja de Santo Ildefonso**, which rises above the Praça da Batalha. The beautiful *azulejos* that adorn the facade were designed in the 1930s by Jorge Calaço – who was responsible for the São Bento station's tiles (see page 42) – though the church, with two distinct bell towers, dates back to the eighteenth century. It was from here that the attempted revolution in 1891 was seen off by municipal guards, who forced the attacking republicans to retreat and eventually surrender from their position at the top of the church steps.

Teatro Nacional São João

MAP PAGE 38, POCKET MAP G6
Praça da Batalha Ⓦ tnsj.pt.
Inspired by Charles Garnier's Opera house in Paris, the **Teatro Nacional São João** is a gorgeously over-the-top building, built in 1911 to replace an earlier theatre that was destroyed in a fire. Today, the city's major theatre and opera venue for Portuguese and international productions, it was renovated in the 1990s after having served as a cinema since the 1930s. The programme is pretty varied and you can see a show for under €10.

Capela das Almas

Jardim de Marquês de Oliveira

MAP PAGE 38, POCKET MAP H5
Entrance on Passeio de São Lázaro. Free.

Tucked away off the tourist route, the attractive **Jardim de Marquês de Oliveira** is a lovely space where elderly men gather to play cards in the shade of beautiful magnolia, linden and cedar trees. The gardens were laid out in 1833 on the site of a former leper colony and formed the city's first-ever public gardens, dotted with fountains and statues, centred around a little lake. Unusually for Portugal, the gardens are railed off and closed at night.

São Bento Station

MAP PAGE 38, POCKET MAP F5
Praça Almeida Garrett.

It is not often that a train station concourse is a sight in its own right, but the one at **São Bento** is one of the most beautiful in the world. Built on the site of a former convent in 1900, it is decorated with around 20,000 sumptuous *azulejos* by painter Jorge Colaço. These show various scenes from Portuguese history, including the visit of Dom João I to Porto in 1387, with his wife Philippa of Lancaster. The towering, ornate ceilings, arched windows and impressive clock all give the appearance of a palace ballroom rather than a ticket hall. The station is the starting point for the fantastic Linha do Douro (see page 37).

Avenida dos Aliados

MAP PAGE 38, POCKET MAP E4–F4
Not quite all roads lead to the **Avenida dos Aliados** (just "Aliados" to locals), but most do. At the foot of the broad avenue – in the area known as Praça da Liberdade – are a couple of pavement cafés and an equestrian statue of Dom Pedro IV; at the head stands the statue of celebrated local boy Almeida Garrett (1799–1854), poet, novelist, dramatist and Liberal politician. Behind the statue at the top of the avenue is Porto's city hall, the **Câmara Municipal**, whose 70m-high clock tower sits at the top of the square. The town hall was designed in 1914 but didn't open until the 1950s. To the left of the town hall as you face it is the city's main tourist office (see page 127).

Porto's specialities

Porto's menus go big on grilled fish, seafood and *bacalhau*, but the most authentic local speciality is *tripas* (tripe) – the story goes that the inhabitants selflessly gave away all their meat for Infante Dom Henrique's expeditions to North Africa, leaving themselves only the tripe, and it's been on the menu ever since, cooked *à moda do Porto* (stewed with *chouriço* and white beans). The other speciality is the **francesinha** ("little French thing") – a mighty chunk of steak, sausage and ham between toasted bread, covered with melted cheese and a peppery tomato-and-beer sauce. It was invented by a café worker called Daniel Silva, who had lived in France and decided to do his own version of their *croque monsieur*. Don't plan on doing anything much after chowing down on either of these Porto belt-tighteners.

Mercado do Bolhão

MAP PAGE 38, POCKET MAP G3–G4
Rua Formosa.

The heartbeat of the busy commercial area around Rua Formosa is the wrought-iron **Mercado do Bolhão**. Built in 1914 and set on two levels, the market has a balcony running round the top that gives it a theatrical air as you peer down over the bustle of stalls. There's been a market on this spot since 1839 and it feels little changed since then, with stalls selling beans by weight, fishmongers gutting their fish in front of you and cages of live chickens, rabbits and pigeons. The historic building itself had been neglected for years but after a much-delayed renovation, the revamped market reopened in 2022. The ground floor houses over eighty traditional stalls and a cluster of specialist shops, while the upper storey has been reimagined as a foodie space for restaurants and culinary events.

Capela das Almas

MAP PAGE 38, POCKET MAP G3
Rua de Santa Catarina 428
222 005 765. Free.

Also known as the chapel of Santa Catarina, the most striking aspect of the early eighteenth-century **Capela das Almas** is its exterior, which is lined with *azulejos* showing scenes from the death of St Francis of Assisi and the Martyrdom of St Catherine. The tiles were designed in 1929 by artist and ceramicist Eduardo Leite, but mimic the style of *azulejos* that were popular in the eighteenth century. There are also stained-glass windows, nineteenth-century embellishments by Amandio Silva.

Estádio do Dragão

MAP PAGE 38
Via Futebol Clube do Porto, Antas, off Av Fernão Magalhães Estádio do Dragão
fcporto.pt. Charge.

The impressive 50,400-capacity **Estádio do Dragão**, 4km northeast of the centre, is home to FC Porto, European champions in 2004 and winners of the Europa League in 2011. Built for the 2004 European Championships, it's a great match venue and rarely sells out. Tickets are available from the club website, the East Stand ticket office or from various shops in town; see website for details. The stadium also hosts major gigs, with Coldplay and the Rolling Stones having played here. You can visit the ground on tours, which leave from outside the club museum. The museum is fascinating if you have an interest in the club's history. You can see FC Porto's array of trophies and watch recordings of past glories, and learn about the club's formation in 1893 by a local wine trader.

Shops

Alameda

MAP PAGE 38
Rua dos Campeões Europeus 28–198
ⓦ alamedashopping.pt.
Close to FC Porto's stadium, this
giant shopping centre is set over
five floors with more than 120
shops, including a Continente
hypermarket, a multi-cinema, a free
car park and various restaurants.

A Pérola do Bolhão

MAP PAGE 38, POCKET MAP G4
Rua Formosa 279 ⓣ 222 004 009.
This great little grocery-café was
founded in 1917 and is loved as
much for its Art Nouveau facade
and its colourful *azulejos* as it is
for its cluttered stock of goods,
ranging from *bacalhau* and port
wine to mountain cheeses, cured
sausages and smoked hams.

Bazar Paris

MAP PAGE 38, POCKET MAP F4
Rua Sá da Bandeira 190 ⓦ bazarparis.pt.
This small, unassuming place is the
oldest toy shop in the city, and is a
good place to find the usual range
of kids' games along with some
lovely vintage retro toys, including
dolls, cars and train sets.

Casa da Guitarra

MAP PAGE 38, POCKET MAP F6
Av Vímara Peres 72 ⓦ casadaguitarra.pt.
Situated on the road leading to the
top tier of Ponte de Dom Luís I, this
space sells and produces beautiful
Portuguese guitars, and by doing so
is working to maintain an ancient
craft. The shop also promotes music
lessons, exhibitions and *Fado às 6h*
concerts (see page 47).

Comer e Chorar Por Mais

MAP PAGE 38, POCKET MAP G4
Rua Formosa 300
ⓦ comerechorarpormais.com.
This shop's name translates as "Eat
and cry for Mum" and you will
be more than tempted to do the

former here: this is a treasure trove
of tasty things to eat and drink,
from its selection of ripe cheeses
and cured hams and sausages to
delicious ports, wines, jams and
other preserves.

Costa Nova

MAP PAGE 38, POCKET MAP G2
Rua de Sá da Bandeira 650 ⓦ costanova.pt.
This uber-chic store specializes in
hand-crafted ceramic tableware
made by Portuguese artisans.
Expect a muted, minimalist vibe,
though the palette does extend to
some vibrant splashes of colour;
the Madeira collection in luminous
teal hues is particularly beautiful.
Also sells table linens, cork coasters,
glassware and placemats.

FNAC

MAP PAGE 38, POCKET MAP G5
Rua de Santa Catarina 73 ⓦ fnac.pt.
This is the most central branch of
this large department store chain
and is the one to head to for the
city's biggest selection of CDs,
DVDs, books, games and gadgets.

Mão Esquerda Vintage

MAP PAGE 38, POCKET MAP H5
Rua de Alegria 5 ⓦ maoesquerda.com.
A wave of excellent vintage shops
is springing up across the Bonfim
neighbourhood, and this thrift
store is one of the best (a little
further out of town, Retro City is
another standout).

Cafés

Café Majestic

MAP PAGE 38, POCKET MAP G4
Rua de Santa Catarina 112
ⓦ cafemajestic.com.
The best-known of the city's Belle
Époque cafés, with perfectly
preserved decor (celestial cherubs,
bevelled mirrors, carved chairs,
wood panelling) and attentive
waiters flitting about to the strains
of *The Blue Danube*. Come for
coffee, afternoon tea or maybe a

Belle Époque beauty *Café Majestic*

light lunch, though you may have to wait for a table at busy times. €€€

Casa Guedes

MAP PAGE 38, POCKET MAP H5
Praça dos Poveiros 130 Ⓦ casaguedes.pt.
This tiny, atmospheric, no-frills tiled café serves some of Porto's tastiest roast pork sandwiches. Queue at the counter to pre-pay, then watch as slabs of juicy pork are piled onto a bread roll – and topped with melted cheese, too, if you want – then head outside to sit at a table overlooking the square. €

Combi Coffee Roasters

MAP PAGE 38
Rua do Morgado de Mateus 29
Ⓣ 914 023 978.
Follow your nose to this independent specialty coffee roastery, where freshly roasted beans are transformed into silky-smooth brews. €

Confeitaria do Bolhão

MAP PAGE 38, POCKET MAP G4
Rua Formosa 339
Ⓦ confeitariadobolhao.com.
Opposite Bolhão market, this wonderful, bustling café, deli and

shop dates back to 1896. The counter is laden with cakes and pasties, such as *pão de deu* (a sweet bread), onion cake and giant *pastel de nata*. It also serves good-value daily set lunches. €

Dama Pé de Cabra

MAP PAGE 38, POCKET MAP H5
Passeio de Sao Lazaro 5 Ⓣ 22 3 196 776.
Looking onto the pretty Jardim de Marques de Oliveira, the oddly named "Woman with a goat's foot" is a great spot for breakfast, lunch or brunch. The team make their own breads, featuring ingredients such as chestnut, pumpkin and carrot, which you can enjoy at breakfast toasted with eggs or homemade jam, or served in a variety of sandwiches for lunch. €

Restaurants

Almeja

MAP PAGE 38, POCKET MAP F4
Rua de Fernandes Tomás 819
Ⓦ almejaporto.com.
Husband-and-wife team João and Sofia Cura are behind this exciting venture – and they've scored a

Michelin listing for their efforts. The Indian-influenced menu is inspired by João's travels in South Asia: think enoki mushroom with black garlic sauce and fermented banana or vegetable curry samosa sprinkled in icing sugar. If you're feeling flush, opt for the ten-course tasting menu. €€€€

Antunes

MAP PAGE 38, POCKET MAP F2
Rua do Bonjardim 525–529 ☎ 222 052 406.
This small local restaurant plates up traditional dishes, such as fantastic meat stews, roast pork, hake with rice and decent steaks, best washed down with a carafe of house *rosado*. €

Conga

MAP PAGE 38, POCKET MAP F4
Rua do Bonjardim 318 ☎ 222 000 113.
Conga opened in 1976 as an unassuming snack-bar and quickly gained a cult following for its *bifana*, a hearty pork sandwich. Since then, it has grown up into a sophisticated (though still relaxed) restaurant. The menu has expanded (though the *bifana* remains its main calling card), and now includes dishes like *papas de sarrabulho*, a cumin-spiked offal stew. €€

Escondidinho

MAP PAGE 38, POCKET MAP G5
Rua Passos Manuel 142 ☯ escondidinho.pt.
Its name means "little hidden one", but with its ornate tiled entrance hall, it's hardly inconspicuous. This upmarket restaurant is barely changed from when it opened in the 1930s, full of wood beams and ceramics. The speciality here is *cataplana*: choose from meat, fish, seafood or a mix. Past guests have included Spanish and Italian royalty, plus famous Portuguese prime ministers Mario Soares and Sá Carneiro. You'll need deep pockets for this one. €€€€

Euskalduna Studio

MAP PAGE 38
R. de Santo Ildefonso 404 ☯ euskaldunastudio.pt.
This sixteen-seat, Michelin-starred restaurant is a favourite among globetrotting gourmands. Chef Vasco Coelho Santos takes the helm in the kitchen, conjuring inventive season-led 'surprise' menus showcasing ingredients from small-scale Portuguese producers. Half the diners sit up at a marble counter, talking to chefs as they prepare that

River-view terraces at *Guindalense Futebol Clube*

evening's tasting menu, creating a relaxed, intimate vibe. €€€€

Flor dos Congregados

MAP PAGE 38, POCKET MAP F5
Trav dos Congredados 11
Ⓦ flordoscongregados.pt.

Tucked down a small back alley, this restaurant dates back to 1852 and claims to have used 1001 traditional recipes. Inside, its stone walls and cosy ambience are as appealing as the menu, chalked up on boards and featuring the likes of tripe, game sausage, tuna steaks and sea bass. €€

Palmeira

MAP PAGE 38, POCKET MAP F4
Rua Ateneu Comercial do Porto 36
Ⓣ 220 055 601.

Handy if you're catching a bus from the Rodonorte bus station opposite, this bustling local has a long menu of good-value fish and meat (*bacalhau*, *pescada*, roast lamb, *alheira* sausage). Join the locals on stools at the bar counter or take a seat in the larger dining room downstairs. €€

Pedro dos Frangos

MAP PAGE 38, POCKET MAP F4
Rua do Bonjardim 223 & 312
Ⓦ pedrodosfrangos.pt.

Places specializing in chargrilled chicken are scarce in central Porto, but this local haunt has been serving bargain *frango na brasa* since the 1950s, served with a heap of chips and salad. It also dishes up octopus, steaks and other grills. The restaurant spreads to both sides of the road: both parts have an upstairs dining room and a downstairs bar area. €

Bars and live music venues

Coliseu do Porto

MAP PAGE 38, POCKET MAP G5
Rua de Passos Manuel 137 Ⓦ coliseu.pt.

The main city-centre venue for international acts, with shows ranging from rock, indie and pop to ballet, classical and musicals.

Guindalense Futebol Clube

MAP PAGE 38, POCKET MAP F7
Escadas dos Guindais 43 Ⓣ 222 034 246.

Begun in 1976 by a group of boys who liked playing football (and are still active in promoting sport among young people), the community-run *Guindalense FC* has a lively cafe-bar, with river-view terraces, pool and babyfoot tables, and cheap food and beer. It's always busy with a young crowd.

Hot Five

MAP PAGE 38, POCKET MAP G7
Largo do Actor Dias 51 Ⓦ hotfive.pt.

Long-established and charismatic jazz club close to the top of the Elevador de Guindais. There are live acts most nights, and though jazz and blues are the staples, it also showcases local talent in different genres. There are two bar areas decorated with black-and-white photos of jazz legends.

Maus Hábitos

MAP PAGE 38, POCKET MAP G5
Rua Passos Manuel 178–4
Ⓦ maushabitos.com.

At the top of an Art Deco car park is "Bad Habits", a late-night, in-crowd venue for alternative music (jazz, funk, indie and world) and contemporary arts. It's not as exclusively hip as you might expect, and out-of-towners are more than welcome. There's a daily veggie lunch, plus regular exhibitions and events in the gallery.

Porto Fado

MAP PAGE 38, POCKET MAP F6
Av Vímara Peres 49 Ⓦ portofado.pt.

Organized by the Casa da Guitarra, these live one-hour *fado às 6h* ("fado at 6") concerts are held in an intimate venue and include a glass of port in the interval. Often feature performances and workshops by top fado guitarists such as Cústodio Castelo.

The Baixa

Although Baixa means "lower town", Porto's commercial heart lies well above the riverfront. Its main sights are the ornate Igreja do Carmo church, famed for its dazzling *azulejos* tiles, the city's best vantage point in the form of the towering Torre dos Clérigos, and the Centro Português de Fotografia, whose location in a former prison is every bit as fascinating as its exhibits. A lively, bustling district that is fun simply to wander around, the Baixa is home to the city's university and has its fair share of cafés, bars, clubs and shops, including one of Europe's most-visited bookshops, the over-the-top Livraria Lello, put firmly on the tourist map by former customer J K Rowling.

Museu da Misericórdia do Porto

MAP PAGE 50, POCKET MAP D6
Rua das Flores 15 Ⓦ mmipo.pt. Charge.

Adjoining the stunning sixteenth-century Igreja da Misericórdia church, this four-storey **museum** is surprisingly interesting. Until 2013, the building was home to the Santa Casa da Misericórdia, one of the country's oldest and largest charities, which was founded over five hundred years ago for philanthropic purposes. The museum's top floor traces the history of the organization, which funded and ran hospitals for the poor, paid for surgeons and lawyers for prisoners, and also built the first orphanage, installed a Braille press for blind people and built a medical school in Porto: look out for the display cabinets housing some of the medical school's original surgical instruments, such as a primitive brain-surgery kit and horrific-looking electric shock therapy equipment. There's also an impressive Gallery of Benefactors, containing paintings of those who provided funds for the charity – the size of each painting corresponds to how much the subject in it donated. The second floor displays the organization's rich collection of religious art, including paintings, sculptures, ornate gold and silver reliquaries, jewellery and vestments embroidered with gold thread – the scale of the treasures gives some idea of the Misericórdia's wealth at its prime. The highlight of the first floor is the *Fons Vitae*, a huge painting by an unknown artist of the Flemish School (around 1520) showing Dom Manuel I with his family kneeling before Christ on the cross. A beautiful iron and glass gallery with a tiled floor leads into the choir of the impressive Baroque Igreja da Misericórdia, which was largely rebuilt in the eighteenth century by Nicolau Nasoni (see page 49). Access to the main chapel, with its stunning tiled nave and beautiful sacristy, is on the ground floor.

Rua das Flores

With its grand wrought-iron balconied buildings and tiled facades, the attractive street of **Rua das Flores** dates back to the sixteenth century when it was laid out on land belonging to Porto's bishop, and named after the existing orchards and gardens. In the nineteenth century, Rua das Flores became Porto's upmarket shopping street, with wealthy traders such as goldsmiths colonizing the northern side and other vendors, like fabric sellers, setting up shop on the south side. However, the street later suffered a decline, and many of its buildings fell into disrepair and were abandoned. Over the past decade, a large-scale regeneration project has seen the street pedestrianized and its beautiful buildings renovated and restored to their former grandeur. New shops, cafés and restaurants have opened up and, today, the street is a real pleasure to stroll down, browsing around the artisan food and craft shops, admiring the colourful tiled facades and lingering for a coffee at one of its many pavement cafés.

Igreja dos Clérigos

Torre dos Clérigos and Igreja dos Clérigos

MAP PAGE 50, POCKET MAP D5
Rua São Filipe Nery
Ⓦ torredosclerigos.pt. Charge.
The best vantage point in the city centre is from the top of the

Baroque **Torre dos Clérigos**, which towers 75m above the streets. This slender finger-like structure was the tallest building in Portugal when it was built in 1763 and,

Porto's historic architecture

Porto's churches provide one of the country's richest concentrations of **Baroque** architecture. The style was brought to Portugal by Italian painter and architect **Nicolau Nasoni** (1691–1773), who arrived in Porto at the age of 34, and remained there for the rest of his life. The church and tower of Clérigos is his greatest work, though his masterful touch can also be seen in the Sé cathedral and adjacent bishop's palace, and at the churches of Misericórdia, Carmo, Santo Ildefonso and São Francisco. All are remarkable for their decorative exuberance, reflecting the wealth derived from Portugal's colonies.

In the second half of the eighteenth century, out went the luxuriant complexity of Baroque and in came the studied lines of the **Neoclassical** period. Neoclassicism also incorporated hints of Gothic and Baroque art, but most of all, was influenced by Islamic style, which reached its apotheosis in the Salão Árabe of the Palácio da Bolsa. By the turn of the twentieth century, Porto's Neoclassicism had acquired a French **Renaissance** touch, thanks largely to the architect **José Marquês da Silva** (1869–1947), who studied in Paris. His most notable works were São Bento station, the exuberant Teatro Nacional São João, and the distinctly less elegant monument to the Peninsular War that dominates the Rotunda da Boavista.

The Baixa

RESTAURANTS

Caldeireiros	8
Cana Verde	7
Cantina 32	11
Cantinho do Avillez	12
Cervejaria Brasão	3
DOP	13
Ernesto	2
Mercador Café	9
Piolho d'Ouro	5
Tascö	4
Xico Queijo	6

CAFÉ

Café Candelabro	1
Mercearia das Flores	10

SHOPS

Arcádia	5
A Vida Portuguesa	6
Chaminé da Mota	9
Chocolataria Ecuador	8
Coração Alecrim	1
Fernandes Mattos & Ca	4
Livraria Lello	3
Lufa Lufa	7
Porto Belo Mercado	2

BARS AND CLUBS

Aduela	3
BASE	8
Casa da Ló	2
Galeria de Paris	5
Páteo da Flores	9
Pipa Velha	1
Plano B	7
Tendinha dos Clérigos	4
The Wall Bar	6

ACCOMMODATION

Duas Nações	4
Grande Hotel Paris by Stay Hotels	5
Infante Sagres	3
OCA Flores Hotel Boutique	7
OCA Vitória Village	6
Pão de Açúcar	2
Pilot Design Hostel	1
Porto Alive	8

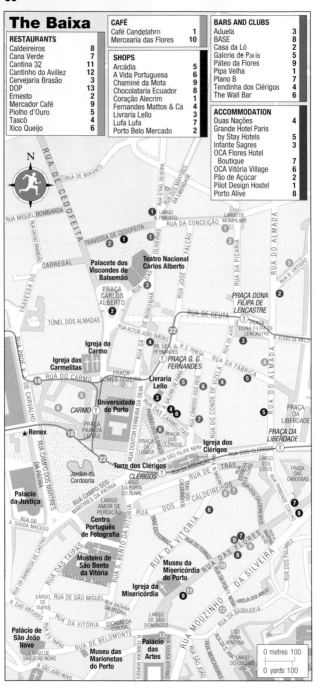

once you've puffed your way up the two hundred-odd stairs, you can enjoy sweeping views from the top. Before you leave, step through the door into the associated church, the **Igreja dos Clérigos** – designed, like the tower, by busy Porto architect Nicolau Nasoni (see box, page 49), who, after half a lifetime spent in his adopted city, was buried in the church at his own request.

Jardim da Cordoaria

MAP PAGE 50, POCKET MAP C5–D5

The main university building in Porto flanks one side of the **Jardim da Cordoaria**, the "Garden of rope-makers", named after the rope-makers who once worked here. It's a lovely space, with gigantic plane trees sheltering huddles of students and old men playing card and chess games. Look out for the statue *Thirteen People Laughing at Each Other*, by Spanish artist Juan Muñoz, which dates from 2001 when Porto was named the European Capital of Culture. There are more monumental buildings on all sides, and a clutch of pavement cafés flanking Praça de Parada Leitão. Two of Porto's trams leave from alongside the gardens, the circular route #22 to Batalha and #18 which runs to the Palácio de Cristal.

Centro Português de Fotografia

MAP PAGE 50, POCKET MAP D6

Largo Amor de Perdição Ⓦ cpf.pt. Free.

The imposing Neoclassical building to the south of the Jardim da Cordoaria – distinguished by 103, mostly barred, windows – was the city's eighteenth-century prison, the Cadeia da Relação. The prison remained in use until the revolution of 1974, but it is now the headquarters of the **Centro Português de Fotografia**, which has restored the building's cells, chambers, workshops and internal courtyards and converted them into extraordinary exhibition spaces. Temporary shows cover anything from vintage Portuguese

photography to contemporary urban work from Brazil and elsewhere.

On the museum's top floor, there is a collection of antique cameras and photographic equipment, from the "stereo-graphoscope" of 1885 to all manner of classic Kodaks and Yashicas. The museum is impressive, though it's the history of the building itself that holds much of the interest. It was built in 1767 in a wedge shape to fit between the old city walls and a convent, and the prisoners were allocated cells according to the severity of their crimes, their status and their ability to pay. The worst offenders were put in damp dungeons accessed by a trap door; women were kept in communal cells on the second floor, while the top-floor "Malta Rooms" were airy individual cells with city views, where "people of status" were only locked in at night. The prison also had its own infirmary, guards' living quarters and a courthouse.

Igreja do Carmo

MAP PAGE 50, POCKET MAP D4

Rua do Carmo Ⓣ 223 322 928. Free.

Beyond the north side of the Jardim da Cordoaria, across from the

Jardim da Cordoaria

Praça de Lisboa

university, the eighteenth-century **Igreja do Carmo** has two instantly recognizable traits – its deliriously over-the-top exterior *azulejos* and the four saints atop the facade, seemingly poised to jump.

Inside, the elegant gilt carvings are among the finest examples of Portuguese Rococo.

Igreja das Carmelitas

MAP PAGE 50, POCKET MAP C4–D4
Rua do Carmo ☎ 222 050 279. Free.
The older and rather more sober **Igreja das Carmelitas** lies almost – but not quite – adjacent to the Igrejo do Carmo because of a law that stipulated that no two churches were to share the same wall (in this case perhaps to hinder amorous liaisons between the nuns of Carmelitas and the monks of Carmo). As a result, what is probably the narrowest house in Portugal – barely 1m wide, and with its own letterbox – was built between them and, though now empty, remained inhabited until the 1980s.

Livraria Lello

MAP PAGE 50, POCKET MAP D5
Rua das Carmelitas 144
Ⓦ livrarialello.pt. Charge for entry, redeemable against any purchase.
Porto's famous galleried Art Nouveau **bookshop**, with its Neo-Gothic exterior and inner staircase just begging for a grand entrance, is a delight beyond words. It was founded by the well-to-do Lello brothers and intellectuals in 1906 and specialized in limited-edition books – many of which are still here (see page 54). The brothers now appear as bas-reliefs on the walls, alongside busts of great writers, including Eça de Queiroz and Cervantes. The Lellos commissioned an engineer and fellow bibliophile Francisco Xavier Esteves to design the interior, which is simply stunning. The ground floor even has rails set into the floor for transporting book "carriages". The impressive double, freestanding staircase (actually made of concrete) lures people upstairs where you can admire the extraordinary plasterwork ceiling, which resembles ornately carved wood.

Columns and a stained-glass roof light add to the air of something far grander than a simple bookshop, the whole design having an almost organic feel, as if the walls and ceiling are the ribs and bones of a living creature. The first floor was the traditional meeting point of artists and intellectuals, and was frequented by J K Rowling during her time in Porto in the 1990s (see box). It is this, and the similarity

J K Rowling's spell in Porto

J K Rowling moved to Porto to teach English in 1991, and it was here that she started writing the *Harry Potter* novels. She married a local journalist, Jorge Arantes, and moved into his mother's apartment in Rua do Duque de Saldanha. They had a daughter in 1993, but separated the same year. Arantes later claimed he had helped come up with ideas for the *Harry Potter* novels, which have earned Rowling more than £600 million – though she denies this. Rowling subsequently returned to Edinburgh with her daughter and the first three chapters of her Harry Potter novel. Her life in Portugal clearly influenced aspects of the books: one of Hogwarts' founding professors was Salazar Slytherin (Salazar being Portugal's notorious dictator for much of the twentieth century), while many of Potter's spells can be easily understood by Portuguese speakers: witness *aguamenti* (bring out water), *duro* (make things hard), *protego* (protect people) and *silencio* (to silence people). There are many similarities, too, between Porto's more characterful buildings and elements of Hogwarts, notably the fantastical decor of the Livraria Lello bookshop (see 52), with its twisting double staircase – though Rowling has always refused to confirm or deny its influence.

of the shop's decor to some of Hogwarts' more outlandish design characteristics, that has put the bookshop firmly on the tourist circuit, with up to four thousand people visiting daily.

There are often queues to get in, but if you come first thing in the morning or in the evening shortly before closing time, you may be able to experience the place more as a bookshop than a tourist site.

Praça de Lisboa

MAP PAGE 50, POCKET MAP D5

The broad **Praça de Lisboa** is one of Porto's most fashionable squares. In the middle of it, you'll find the Passeio dos Clérigos, a mini shopping mall beneath a concrete mantel, all neatly landscaped on top with lawns and gnarled olive trees. Just off the square, Rua Cândido dos Reis is lined with handsome Art Nouveau buildings, laid out in the early nineteenth century after the demolition of an old convent. It's now the hub of Porto's nightlife scene, flanked by clubs and bars, and also hosts

a crafts market on the second and last Saturday of the month.

Palacete dos Viscondes de Balsemão

MAP PAGE 50, POCKET MAP D4
Praça Carlos Alberta 71
⊕ 223 393 480. Free.

Built in the nineteenth century for the wealthy Godinho family, and briefly home to the exiled King of Sardinia, this small **palace** now houses an exhibition centre in two of its rooms. One hosts temporary exhibits, the other an interesting collection of historic coins, including some dating back to the birth of the country. Adjacent to the palace, a separate exhibition space, The Bank of Materials, displays important materials salvaged by the town council from historic buildings.

There's a range of beautiful *azulejos* dating from the fifteenth century, mostly taken from building facades, along with a collection of historic street signs and roof tiles – it's certainly worth a browse on a wet day.

Shops

Arcádia

MAP PAGE 50, POCKET MAP E5
Rua do Almada 63
Ⓦ arcadiachocolates.com.

The Bastos family has been making chocolate in Porto since 1933, using top-quality natural ingredients. There are several branches around the city now (including one at Rua de Santa Catarina 191), but this is the original, with its blue-tiled walls and wooden interior. The chocolates are delicious and come in a variety of tantalizing and creative flavours, including cinnamon and ginger, tangerine and, of course, port.

A Vida Portuguesa

MAP PAGE 50, POCKET MAP D5
Galeria de Paris 20
Ⓦ avidaportuguesa.com.

Everything at this enchanting shop is the work of Portuguese makers who pride themselves on honouring age-old traditions. Shelves are adorned with beautiful displays of hand-embroidered textiles, artist-designed stationery, books, toiletries and tableware, all rooted in place. You can pick up stunning souvenirs here, such as linen placemats etched with traditional floral patterns or nostalgia-seeped items like shaving cream from a 1920s product line and bundles of early-twentieth-century graphite pencils.

Chaminé da Mota

MAP PAGE 50, POCKET MAP D6
Rua das Flores 28 ☏ 222 005 380.

Founded in 1981, this charming store is an Aladdin's cave of old books and objects, including rare tomes, magazines, ancient radios and record players, posters and even a mini printing press. You may not necessarily want to buy anything, but it's a fascinating place to wander around and listen to the giant music boxes that play when you put €2 in.

Chocolataria Ecuador

MAP PAGE 50, POCKET MAP E5
Rua das Flores 298 Ⓦ cacaoequador.pt.

This tiny shop sells the city's best chocolate, with a top-quality selection of artisan chocolates sold by weight – they come in a variety of flavours, including praline and Jamaican pepper, and mango. The blocks of chocolate are sublime, too – try the dark chocolate with curry or dark chocolate with port. There's a second (larger) branch at Rua Sá da Bandeira 637.

Coração Alecrim

MAP PAGE 50, POCKET MAP D3
Trav de Cedofeita 28
Ⓦ coracaoalecrim.com.

Enticing shop selling local handmade textiles, clothes, jewellery, ceramics and plants, as well as eco-friendly and sustainable vintage-style and designer clothing and homeware.

Fernandes Mattos & Ca

MAP PAGE 50, POCKET MAP D5
Rua dos Carmelitas 108–114
Ⓦ fernandesmattos.pt.

On the ground floor of a lovely old building, this shop started life in 1886 as a fabric store. It still has the traditional wooden floors, shelves and cabinets, but today it sells all kinds of retro and vintage-style artefacts, such as posters, games, toys and biscuit tins, as well as more contemporary mugs and rucksacks. Upstairs on the first floor, a branch of A Vida Portuguesa sells traditional ceramics, textiles and soaps.

Livraria Lello

MAP PAGE 50, POCKET MAP D5
Rua das Carmelitas 144 ☏ 222 002 037.

Porto's famous galleried Art Nouveau remains has become a tourist sight in its own right (see page 52), but behind the crowds this remains one of the city's best bookshops. There's general fiction on the ground floor (including, of course, the *Harry Potter* stories in many different languages), much of it in English, with reference and non-fiction (including travel) on the upper floor. You can also find rare editions of Portuguese books. Look out, too, for the original till, made in 1881, the first in Portugal to issue paper receipts and with prices in reis (the currency before the escudo). You'll get your entry fee back on any purchase.

Lufa Lufa

MAP PAGE 50, POCKET MAP E5
Rua das Flores 191 ⓦ lufalufa.pt.
Small shop specializing in organic, locally designed cotton T-shirts, with innovative Porto-themed logos (for example, Porto written to resemble a bicycle).

Porto Belo Mercado

MAP PAGE 50, POCKET MAP D4
Praça Carlos Alberto.
This small market has stallholders selling everything from LPs and old toys to local handicrafts and home-made food. Its name, meaning beautiful Porto, is a nod to London's well-known, and considerably larger, market.

Cafés

Café Candelabro

MAP PAGE 50, POCKET MAP E3
Rua da Conceição 3
ⓦ cafecandelabro.com.
This is a very popular café-bar and bookshop full of old typewriters and photography and art books, which you can purchase or read at the tables. Unsurprisingly, it attracts an arty crowd and morphs into a hip bar in the evenings. Your food options are limited to snacks and nibbles, but it serves a mean gin 'n' tonic and chilled glass of *vinho verde*. €

Mercearia das Flores

MAP PAGE 50, POCKET MAP E6
Rua das Flores 110
ⓦ merceariadasflores.com.
This lovely little deli/café sells regional and organic produce, including tinned fish of all descriptions, olive oils and wines. It's a great place to browse or you can settle down at the tables in the pedestrianized street for a coffee and cake, or for lunch – try the toasted sandwich of local sheep's cheese with honey and almonds, or opt for a platter of regional cheese and meats. €

Mercearia das Flores

Restaurants

Caldeireiros

MAP PAGE 50, POCKET MAP E5
Rua dos Caldeireiros 139 ☎ 223 214 074.
With stylish but simple decor –
the plain painted walls are dotted
with colourful tiles and mini-
chandeliers hang from the ceiling
– this long, thin restaurant has
communal bench tables and serves
tasty and reasonably priced food.
The menu features a selection of
tapas, plus main courses such as
filletes de pescada or a Mirandese
steak. It also offers a half-portion
francesinho – a good idea if
you want to sample this hearty
Porto speciality without feeling
completely stuffed afterwards. €

Cana Verde

MAP PAGE 50, POCKET MAP E5
Rua dos Caldeireiros 121 ☎ 222 018 042.
Locals queue outside this tiny
restaurant, with its blue-tiled
walls and few tables on the street,
for the cheap and cheerful filling

Creative cuisine at *DOP*

lunchtime dishes. Expect large,
good-value plates piled with
traditional dishes such as *filletes
de pescada*, grilled chicken or
febras are all accompanied by tasty
tomato rice. Meanwhile, the set
lunch is a steal, with soup, bread,
dish of the day and a coffee for
under €10. €

Cantina 32

MAP PAGE 50, POCKET MAP D6
Rua das Flores 32 ☎ 222 039 069.
With its industrial-style interior,
long bench tables and seating
spilling outside on the street, this
is a good spot for a quick snack
and a drink or to linger for a full
meal. The *petiscos* are tasty – try the
bacalhau, or carpaccio with truffle
sauce – while main courses include
the likes of squid and shrimp stew
or tiger prawns with lashings of
garlic butter. €€

Cantinho do Avillez

MAP PAGE 50, POCKET MAP E6
Rua Mouzinha da Silveira 166
ⓦ cantinhodoavillez.pt.
Michelin-starred chef José Avillez's
first Porto outlet, *Cantinho do
Avillez*, is an excellent place to
sample top-quality and inventive
Portuguese food at surprisingly
affordable prices. This welcoming
restaurant, with a tiled floor and
retro-style decor, may be laidback
and informal, but the food is
innovative and interesting, with
Avillez's playful spin on Portuguese
classics – sample the likes of
lightly cooked tuna, scallops, game
sausage and his famous burgers,
not to mention the signature
exploding olives. €€€€

Cervejaria Brasão

MAP PAGE 50, POCKET MAP E3
Rua de Ramalho Ortigão 28 ⓦ brasao.pt.
This modern twist on an old-
fashioned *cervejaria* (beer hall),
is hugely popular with locals
and tourists. As well as decent
beer, you'll find a range of snacky
food, including *pregos* (steak

sandwiches), *francesinhos* and
petiscos. There are also mains,
including sumptuous steaks. €€€

DOP

MAP PAGE 50, POCKET MAP D6
Palácio das Artes, Largo São Domingos 18
Ⓦ doprestaurante.pt.
Come here to see well-known Porto
chef Rui Paula wow punters with
the creative Portuguese cuisine that
made his name (see page 78).
Expect a playful twist on traditional
cuisine, such as veal cheek with
gnocchi or lamb with goat cheese
purée – at a price, mind you.
You should be able to rock up for
lunch, but in the evening, dinner
reservations are advised. €€€€

Ernesto

MAP PAGE 50, POCKET MAP E3
Rua da Picaria 85 ☎ 222 002 600.
A pleasantly old-fashioned
restaurant dating back to the
1930s, which proudly displays an
autographed menu from Bono of
U2. The regional food is excellent,
with the menu usually featuring
the likes of roast goat, veal, octopus
and *bacalhau*, along with the fresh
fish of the day. €€€

Mercador Café

MAP PAGE 50, POCKET MAP 56
Rua das Flores 180 Ⓦ mercadorcafe.pt.
Airy, high-ceilinged café in an
old fabric store, with the original
wooden cabinets inside and tables
on the street in front. It serves
pastries, coffees and lunch, as
well as more substantial dishes
such as pork with asparagus and
port sauce. There's usually also a
budget-friendly dish of the day,
which changes regularly, but may
well feature the likes of cod and
onions, or mushroom risotto with
duck. €€€

Piolho d'Ouro

MAP PAGE 50, POCKET MAP C5
Praça Parada Leitão 43–55 ☎ 222 003 749.
Since 1909, this no-frills
traditional café-restaurant has been

BASE café-bar atop Passeio dos Clérigos

serving students from the nearby
university with large, cheap plates
of food. Always busy, it has dark
wooden furniture, football on the
TV most nights and tables out on
the square. Good for a coffee or
drink, it also does soups, salads and
sandwiches plus large portions of
pescada or *febras*. €€

Tascö

MAP PAGE 50, POCKET MAP E4
Rua do Almada 151A Ⓦotasco.pt/en.
With low lighting and warm wood
accents, this inviting restaurant is
the place to go for *petiscos*. Order
a feast for the table to share:
bacalhau, tomato rice, paprika-
spiked *alheira* (sausage), garlicky
sautéed potatoes, all washed down
with a bottle of *vinho verde*. Save
room, though, for a serving of
delicious home-made ice cream for
dessert. €€€

Xico Queijo

MAP PAGE 50, POCKET MAP C5
Galeria de Paris 79 ☎ 223 164 000.
Smack bang on one of Porto's
liveliest streets, this glass-
fronted haunt spills out onto the
pavement, both its indoor and

outdoor tables filled with diners lingering over sharing platters of Portuguese meats and cheeses. Order the house sangria or one of the signature cocktails – perhaps the Xico Shaker, a punchy mix of vodka, orange and lemon juice, lime and ginger. €€€

Bars and clubs

Aduela

MAP PAGE 50, POCKET MAP D4
Rua das Oliveiras 36 ☎ 222 084 398.
A traditional bar that is now very on trend, with outdoor seating shaded beneath a gnarled olive tree. There's a good range of wines, mojitos and sangria, as well as inexpensive snacks.

BASE

MAP PAGE 50, POCKET MAP D5
Jardim dos Clérigos, Praça de Lisboa
ⓦ baseporto.com.
Perched on the grassed-over concrete top of the Passeio dos Clérigos shopping mall, this is a hip café-bar serving hot and cold drinks, including a fine range of cocktails. Take a seat on

the communal wooden benches beneath the umbrellas, surrounded by olive trees.

Casa da Ló

MAP PAGE 50, POCKET MAP D3
Tv do Cedofeita 20a ☎ 220 119 738.
This rustic-chic former bakery has been converted into an enticing bar; the old marble bar a nod to its earlier identity. The space is spread across two rooms filled with wooden tables and opens onto a small courtyard at the back. It's a great place to chill out over a drink during the week, and the pace slips up a few gears come Friday thanks to regular DJ sets at weekends.

Galeria de Paris

MAP PAGE 50, POCKET MAP D4
Rua Galeria de Paris 36 ☎ 222 016 218.
This bar-café has an eclectic collection of things hanging on its walls, including a Fiat car, guitars, dolls and even a toilet. It's a quirky, fun place, with live music in the evenings ranging from fado to pop, and belly-dancing performances. The food is good, with fish dishes, steak and pork chops and some veggie options too.

Plano B

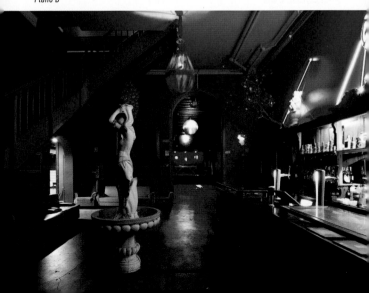

Tendinha dos Clérigos

Páteo da Flores

MAP PAGE 50, POCKET MAP E6
Rua das Flores 135 ℹ 222 031 128.
This friendly wine/tapas bar may
look small from the street, but it
opens out onto an inviting tiled
patio at the back, covered by a
dramatic glass roof. It's a great place
to sample some of the wines on
its extensive list accompanied by
a selection of tapas, such as tasty
padron peppers or a sharing platter.

Pipa Velha

MAP PAGE 50, POCKET MAP D3
Rua das Oliveiras 75 ℹ 223 222 780.
Long-established, laidback bar with
old theatre posters on the walls.
It's a good spot for drinks, as well
as inexpensive *petiscos*, including a
fine flaming *choriço*.

Plano B

MAP PAGE 50, POCKET MAP D5
Rua Cândido dos Reis 30
ⓦ planobporto.com.
Swanky, fashionable and spacious
club, with two dance floors, regular
local and international DJ sessions
and occasional live music, too.
There's an upstairs bar for when
things get too frenetic downstairs,
and a rather grand Greek-style
statue by the downstairs bar. On
Friday and Saturday nights, there
may be an entrance fee, depending
on who's playing.

Tendinha dos Clérigos

MAP PAGE 50, POCKET MAP E4
Rua Conde Vizela 80
ⓦ tendinhadosclerigos.com.
A cave-like bar and club with a
pool table and dance floor, this is
also a regular venue for DJs and
up-and-coming bands. It's the place
to go when all the other bars have
closed for the night, so best to
arrive before 4am unless you like it
truly frenetic.

The Wall Bar

MAP PAGE 50, POCKET MAP D4
Rua Cândido dos Reis 90 ℹ 222 086 557.
One of the hippest nightspots on
the fashionable Rua Cândido dos
Reis – its name comes from the
wacky wall of drinks behind the bar
on one side and a map of the world
made up of country names on the
other. It doesn't get going much
before midnight, after which it can
be packed. Expect good sounds and
a fine range of cocktails.

Vila Nova de Gaia

Though Porto lent its name to port, it's Vila Nova de Gaia, on the opposite bank of the Douro, which is the birthplace of the city's famous drink. Here, a string of port wine lodges grew up in the twelfth century because of the suitably humid conditions – and it continues to dominate the steep slopes of the southern riverfront today. No visit to the city is complete without a tour or tasting at a historic lodge, although Gaia also has plenty of other attractions. Its waterfront cable car offers fantastic views over historic Porto, with even better vistas from the hilltop Mosteiro de Serra do Pilar, and the WOW cultural complex is well worth a visit. Harder to reach, but worth seeking out are the engaging house museum, Casa-Museu Teixeira Lopes, and the city's main zoo, Santo Inácio.

The riverfront

Facing Porto's Ribeira, Vila Nova de Gaia's pretty **riverfront** is a real pleasure to stroll along – with its long line of cafés, bars and restaurants, and wooden artisan stalls selling souvenirs. The cable car glides silently overhead, cruise boats dock alongside the esplanade, while

Vila Nova de Gaia's pretty riverfront

the wooden boats with sails, known as *barcos rabelos*, moor out in the river: cormorants dry themselves on the rudders of these traditional boats, which were once used to transport wine casks downriver from the Douro port estates.

The views are, if anything, better from Vila Nova de Gaia than from the Porto side, as they look back across to a largely eighteenth-century cityscape, with few modern buildings intruding in on the panoramic sweep from the Palácio de Cristal gardens in the west, the Ribeira district and Torre de Cleigos straight ahead and the cathedral towers and Ponte de Dom Luís I to the east.

Teleférico de Gaia

MAP PAGE 62, POCKET MAP D9
Lower station at Cais de Gaia, upper station at Ⓜ Jardim do Morro Ⓦ gaiacablecar.com. Charge.

A good way to explore Gaia – and to take some dramatic aerial shots of Porto and the river – is to ride the **Teleférico de Gaia**, or cable car. Connecting the upper station at the Jardim de Morro, near the top level of the

Getting to Vila Nova de Gaia

There are various ways of getting over the river to Vila Nova de Gaia, depending on where you are starting from. If you are on the Ribeira riverfront, you can simply **walk** over the lower level of the Ponte de Dom Luís I – a ten-minute walk with the bonus of good views en route. Alternatively, you can take the Douro **river taxi**, which takes five minutes to shuttle across the river from the Cais de Estiva to Gaia's riverfront (daily 10am–sunset every 15 minutes or so; ⓦ dourorivertaxi.com). If you're in Porto's upper town, you can take **buses** #900, #901 and #906 from São Bento station across the bridge and along the Gaia riverfront. Alternatively, you can either walk across the upper level of the bridge to the Jardim de Morro, or take **metro** Line D from ⓜ Aliados/São Bento to ⓜ Jardim do Morro; from here, you can take the Teleférico de Gaia or walk down to the riverfront.

Ponte de Dom Luís I, with the far end of the Gaia riverside, the five-minute, 600m-long journey sweeps right above the rooftops of Vila Nova de Gaia's historic port wine lodges.

Mosteiro de Serra do Pilar

MAP PAGE 62, POCKET MAP F9–G9
Largo de Avis ⓣ 220 142 425. Charge.
Spread along the hilltop above Vila Nova de Gaia, the **Moistero de Serra do Pilar** is remarkable for its circular design. Originally modelled on Rome's church of Santa Maria de Redondo, it is the only church in Portugal to have a circular vault and cloisters. The Moistero de Serra de Pilar was built in the sixteenth century for the Order of St Augustine, but its construction lasted over 70 years, during which time Portugal was taken over by the Spanish – hence the monastery being named after a Spanish saint. The monastery was requisitioned by the military during the nineteenth century, with first Wellington, then Napoleon billeting their troops at its defensive heights.

Today, protected by UNESCO World Heritage status, the church offers fantastic views over the river and city from the terrace outside. However, those with a head for heights can take in an even more impressive view by signing up for a guided tour (approximately hourly; except Sunday morning) up to the top of the dome.

On the tour, guides lead you up the 104 steps to walk around a narrow balcony that runs around the outside of the dome: all the tours are escorted by a soldier, since the monastery still belongs to the military.

Jardim do Morro

Next to cable car's upper exit, and accessible from central Porto by walking over the top tier of the Ponte de Dom Luís I or taking the metro to **Jardim do Morro**, these small gardens sit on a hillock above the river, with great views back over town. The lawns and shady palms make this a relaxing place to hang out and a popular spot to watch the sun rise.

Igreja de Santa Marinha

MAP PAGE 62
Largo Santa Marinha. No set opening times.
This is one of Vila Nova de Gaia's oldest churches, remodelled in the seventeenth century by Nicolau Nasoni (see page 49) on the site of a fifteenth-century temple. There are beautiful *azulejos* above the altar and the usual Baroque

flourishes, though the church is often kept locked.

Zoo Santo Inácio

MAP PAGE 62
Rua 5 de Outubro 4503, Avintes
Ⓦ zoosantoinacio.com. Charge.

The small, well-run **Zoo Santo Inácio** houses some eight hundred animals, including lions, giraffes, water buffaloes and Siberian tigers. All the animals here are living in enclosed spaces designed to be as close to their natural habitat as possible. The zoo houses many endangered species, including the snow leopard, and has an active breeding programme to try and improve the numbers of vulnerable species.

Throughout the day there are various demonstrations and feeding sessions, but the highlight is the glass walk-through tunnel in the Asian lions' cage.

Casa-Museu Teixeira Lopes

MAP PAGE 62
Rua de Teixeira Lopes 32 Ⓣ 351 223 751 224; Ⓜ Camara de Gaia. Free.

The **Casa-Museu Teixeira Lopes** is interesting on two levels – first, for its large collection of works by sculptor António Teixeira Lopes (1866–1942) and, secondly, for its insight into life in a wealthy late-nineteenth-century house. The house was built in 1895 by Teixeira Lopes' brother, architect José Teixeira Lopes, as a residence and studio, and has been restored to its former condition. You enter through a pretty garden dotted with sculptures and trees and with views over to the city, then pass through a series of restored rooms, including Teixeira's bedroom, office and dining room, all furnished with the sculptor's personal effects and

ACCOMMODATION	
House of Sandeman	1
The Yeatman	2

SHOPS	
3+ ARTE	2
Casa do Galo	1
El Corte Inglés	3

BARS, NIGHTLIFE & PORT TASTINGS	
Caves Cálem	2
Dick's Bar	6
Kopke House	1
Terrace Lounge 360	3
Quevedo Cellar	5
Sogevinus	4

CAFÉS & RESTAURANTS	
3+ ARTE	9
Barão de Fladgate	10
Beira Rio	5
Casa Adão	8
Casa Dias	7
De Castro	4
Dourum	1
Taberninha do Manel	2
Toca do Coelho	6
Vinum	3
The Yeatman	11

Vila Nova de Gaia

family paintings. A balconied gallery looks down onto Teixeira's vast well-lit studio, while a connecting door leads through to the Diogo de Macedo galleries. These contain works by Diogo de Macedo (1889–1959), a student of Teixeira Lopes, who was born in Vila Nova de Gaia then went on to become the director of Lisbon's Contemporary Art Museum. The collection contains a selection of Macedo's sculptures in a variety of styles as well as some of his personal collection of contemporary paintings and sculptures, including works by Carlos Botelho and Amadeo de Souza Cardoso. The tour ends in Teixeira's studio, with beautiful blue-tiled walls, amid his sculptures cast in bronze and marble and several giant plaster models. Guided tours of the museum are mandatory: you don't have to book, but it's

The circular Moistero de Serra do Pilar

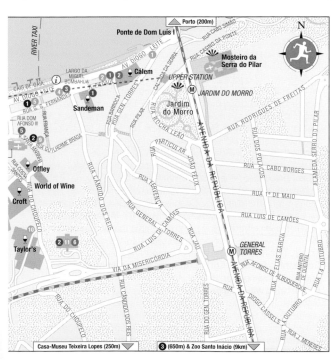

a good idea to phone ahead to check if an English-speaking guide is available.

Port wine lodges

Vila Nova de Gaia's *raison d'être*, of course, is the **port wine trade** – you can't miss the dozens of historic company lodges and warehouses (known as *caves*) that splash their brand names across every rooftop, facade and advertising hoarding. They almost all offer **tastings and tours**, conducted in a variety of languages (including English), with a view to enticing you to buy. Tours of the smaller, lesser-known companies tend to be more personal than those of larger producers, but they are all informative and you'll soon know the difference between a tawny and a ruby, and which vintages are best.

Around thirty **port wine lodges** in Vila Nova de Gaia are open for tastings. Many of the lodges are no longer independent but are owned by a parent company: Kopke, Burmester, Cálem and Barros, for example, belong to the Sogevinus brand, while Graham's, Cockburn's, Dow and Warre all belong to the Symington family, and Sogrape is the parent company of Offley, Ferreira and Sandeman. Most of the lodges are open daily all year round, though some close in the winter: almost all charge a fee for their tours, with the price depending on the ports chosen for the tastings – if you want to taste more ports and some of the pricier vintages, you'll pay extra. Most lodges run a system whereby you can just turn up for a tour, though this will be run in the language of the first person to book onto the tour. If you find that the next tour isn't in English, you may

The port wine story

For three centuries, wine from Portugal's Douro region has been shipped down the river to Vila Nova de Gaia, whose famous wine lodges (Sandeman, Graham's, Cockburn and Taylor's) reflect the early British influence on its production. A **cellar tour** here forms an integral part of any Porto visit, and you can also follow the wine trail inland along the Douro by train, car or cruise boat (see page 127). To find out more, the country's port wine institute, the Instituto dos Vinhos do Douro e do Porto (ⓦ ivdp.pt), has a useful English-language website, while the Rota do Vinho do Porto details the region's wine estates, attractions and events.

The clear distinction between **port wine** (vinho do porto) and other Portuguese wines wasn't made until the beginning of the eighteenth century, when Britain prohibited the import of French wines during the War of the Spanish Succession. Portuguese wines quickly filled the void and, following the **Methuen Treaty** (1703), the wine trade became so profitable that adulterated inferior wines were soon being passed off as the genuine article. This led to the creation of a regulatory body in 1756, the **Companhia Geral da Agricultura das Vinhas do Alto Douro**, and, the following year, the declaration of the world's oldest **demarcated wine region** (where port wine could now only legitimately be produced). Yet it wasn't until the mid-nineteenth century that it began to resemble today's fortified wine, when the addition of brandy to stop fermentation became widespread, enabling the wines to be transported over even longer distances.

Croft, the oldest working port lodge in Porto

have to wait or book (in person or via the websites) onto a later tour.

If you don't have time for a full tour, there are several places that are not actual lodges, but do **port tastings**, including Sogevinus, Kopke House and Quevedo Cellar (see page 70). Some of these do chocolate and olive oil tastings, too, so you can skip all the historical stuff and just head straight for the sofas for some sampling.

Cálem

MAP PAGE 62, POCKET MAP E9–F9
Av Diogo Leite 344 ⓦ calem.pt. Charge.
The nearest port wine lodge to the bridge, and therefore one of the most visited, **Cálem** nevertheless has a good visitor centre, and is especially informative about port wine's history and production process – you can even watch a video about port from inside a vast converted oak vat. Tours last about 45 minutes and start in the lodge museum, then proceed through the cellars, ending with the tasting. Pre-book if you want to make sure you get an English-language tour. It also holds fado concerts in the cellars (see page 71).

Churchill's

MAP PAGE 62, POCKET MAP A8–B8
Rua do Fonte Nova 5
ⓦ churchills-port.com. Charge.
One of the smallest lodges, offering the least expensive and shortest tours (20min), but a good choice if you want a basic background to the production process and the chance to sample a few different ports.

Croft

MAP PAGE 62
Rua Barão de Forrester
ⓦ croftport.com. Charge.
Founded in 1588, Croft is the oldest company still making port today. The short thirty-minute tour of the lodge is led by well-informed guides who take you round the old cellars. You can try a few ports either in an atmospheric tasting room or on the small terrace in summer, which has fine views over the other lodges.

Ferreira

MAP PAGE 62, POCKET MAP B9
Av Ramos Pinto 70
ⓦ eng.sograpevinhos.com. Charge.
The only major port house to have remained wholly under Portuguese

The still-working cellars at Graham's

husband died) until her death in 1896. After a thirty- to forty-minute tour of the cellars, where you can marvel at the giant vats, tastings (two ports) take place in a cavernous vaulted room.

Graham's

MAP PAGE 62, POCKET MAP A9
Rua do Agro 141
Ⓦ grahams-port.com. Charge.

It's a steep walk up to Graham's, which was originally founded by a Scottish family, and is now owned by the Anglo/Scottish/Portuguese Symington wine dynasty. The thirty- to forty-minute tour includes a video and slide show, plus a visit to a light and airy museum with interesting artefacts on display such as one of Winston Churchill's invoices showing his fondness for port and an 1887 Patek Phillippe watch made for the Queen of Portugal. The still-working cavernous cellars below house some two thousand barrels of ageing port, plus numerous bottles of the vintage stuff. The tour ends in the splendid tasting room with great

control, Ferreira was founded in 1751, and is unusual in that it was a woman who was responsible for much of the company's success. Antónia Adelaide Ferreira, known as Ferreirinha, ran the company from the age of 33 (when her first

The Douro wine route

Portugal's port wine grapes are grown in a 600,000-acre demarcated region along both banks of the Rio Douro, stretching from Mesão Frio (near Peso da Régua) to the Spanish border. Sheltered by the Marão and Montemuro mountain ranges, around fifteen percent of the region is under vines, which benefit from cold winters and hot, dry summers. The characteristic terraces can be seen along the length of the Douro, and they form a beautiful backdrop to the small town of Pinhão, which is now the main centre for quality ports. The grapes are harvested at the *quintas* (vineyard estates) from September to October and are then crushed. After a few days, fermentation is halted by the addition of brandy – exactly when this is done determines the wine's sweetness – with the wine subsequently stored in casks until the following March. The final stage in the wine process is its transportation downstream to the shippers' lodges, where the wine is blended and matured. One of the most scenic ways to visit the wine route is by train, along the Linha do Douro (see page 37), while drivers can follow the useful map at Ⓦ dourowinetourism.com, which details wine lodges to visit and *quintas* to stay at. River cruises along the Douro are detailed in Essentials (see page 127).

views and a terrace overlooking the river. The lodge is also home to the highly rated *Vinum* restaurant (see page 70).

Offley

MAP PAGE 62
Rua do Choupelo 54
Ⓦ eng.sograpevinhos.com. Charge.
Although the company was founded in 1737 by William Offley, the man who most influenced it was Joseph James Forrester, later Baron de Forrester, an English wine merchant who ran the company from the 1830s. Although it's not open year-round, this is one of the cheapest lodges to visit: cellar tours with a tasting of two ports cost around €15–20, though if you want to try more ports you can take the Reserve or Baron of Forrester tours.

Ramos Pinto

MAP PAGE 62, POCKET MAP D9
Av Ramos Pinto 400 Ⓦ ramospinto.pt. Charge.
In an attractive riverside building dating from 1880, this distinctive port lodge has a good museum housed in its 1930s period offices – here, you can learn about the history of this Portuguese company whose famous advertising posters did much to popularize port in the 1900s. One of the cheapest lodges, its tours include a trip to the extensive cellars where the port is aged and end, of course, with a tasting session. Tours leave every forty minutes or so, last around forty minutes, and can be booked at the visitor centre.

Sandeman

MAP PAGE 62, POCKET MAP E9
Sandeman Terrace, Largo Miguel Bombarda
Ⓦ sandeman.eu. Charge.
The black-hat-and-cape cut-out provides the most recognizable of company logos and this ancient company certainly makes the most of its figure, with its tour guides dressed up as the distinctive Sandeman Don. In summer, drinks

and food are served on a pleasant riverfront terrace in the front of the lodge. Tours range from a thirty-minute tour including a tasting of two ports, to the 1790 tour (45min–1hr) and sample a handful of ports of a higher quality. It's best to book to ensure an English-language tour.

Taylor's

MAP PAGE 62
Rua do Choupelo 250 Ⓦ taylor.pt. Charge.
Founded in 1692, and still an independent family firm, Taylor's provides an entertaining self-guided audio-tour (roughly 1hr) of its three-hundred-year-old cellars, renovated to include some modern and informative museum exhibits. The tour ends with a port tasting, either in the attractive tasting room or in the pretty gardens and terrace with its panoramic views over the city: if you want to linger further over the view, or sample more of its offerings, you can linger over a meal at the *Barão de Fladgate* restaurant (see page 68).

World of Wine (WOW)

MAP PAGE 62
Rua do Choupelo 39 Ⓦ wow.pt. Charge.
A new museum complex opened its doors in Vila Nova de Gaia in 2020, as part of a mammoth project to transform the city's former wine warehouse district into a cultural quarter. It took five years of renovation works and a cost of €105m (£95m) to launch the **World of Wine (WOW)**, a sprawling hub spread across 55,000sq metres of restored port cellars. Arranged around an open-air square, WOW includes seven museums, five restaurants, shops, bars, event spaces, exhibitions halls and even a wine school offering short courses focusing on Portuguese viticulture and gastronomy. In addition to the temple to wine, the other immersive experiences provide an insight into the key industries, from cork to chocolate and textiles, that make up the fabric of the country.

VILA NOVA DE GAIA

Shops

3+ ARTE

MAP PAGE 62
Largo Joaquim Magalhães 12
☎ 223 758 255.

As well as being an appealing café, this is also a gallery and shop selling work by local artists in an old warehouse, with a caravan operating as its office.

Casa do Galo

MAP PAGE 62, POCKET MAP D9
Av Diogo Leite 50 ☎ 910 657 172.

Arts and crafts shop selling locally designed ceramics and woodcarvings as well as tasteful cork bags and jewellery. It also does port tastings.

El Corte Inglés

MAP PAGE 62
Av da República 1435 ⓦ elcorteingles.pt;
ⓜ Estação João de Deus.

Vast modern Spanish department store with six floors above ground and five below, selling pretty much anything you can think of. There's also an excellent supermarket. The café on the sixth floor is a good-value place for lunch with excellent views over the city.

Café

3+ ARTE

MAP PAGE 62
Largo Joaquim Magalhães 12
☎ 223 758 255.

At the bottom of the hill from *The Yeatman* (see page 70), this delightful tiny café-bar is technically more a multi-purpose community organization that sells local arts and crafts (see above), rescues cats, hires out bikes and also serves wine and tapas. It's a perfect spot for a small lunchtime snack or to indulge your creative side over a glass of wine. €

Restaurants

Barão de Fladgate

MAP PAGE 62
Taylor's, Rua do Choupelo 250
ⓦ baraoffladgate.com.

It's a punishing uphill hike to get here (unless you take a taxi), but when you arrive, you're rewarded by the finest river and bridge views from the terrace of Taylor's port wine lodge restaurant – it's a lovely spot for an alfresco lunch. A fleet of smart waiters is on hand, but it's not stuffily formal and not outrageously expensive either. Many dishes have a slug of port in the recipe, while others (like duck leg with citrus risotto) make a change from the prevailing traditional Portuguese cuisine. €€€€

Beira Rio

MAP PAGE 62, POCKET MAP D9
Av Diogo Leite 64 ⓦ mercadobeirario.pt.

This appealing local restaurant is tiny inside but has tables outside on the riverfront and friendly staff. It serves up local dishes, many simply grilled on the barbecue, such as chicken and sardines or salmon, as well as the ubiquitous hearty *francesinha*. €€€

Casa Adão

MAP PAGE 62, POCKET MAP C9
Av Ramos Pinto 252 ☎ 223 750 492.

Simple family-run riverfront restaurant with low prices for grilled meat and fish, with dishes ranging from steak and pork to salmon and sea bass. It also serves bigger platters of mixed grilled fish and the like for two or more people. Locals pack the place out at lunch, so there might be a wait for a table. €€€€

Casa Dias

MAP PAGE 62, POCKET MAP C9
Av Ramos Pinto 242 ☎ 223 750 467.

Casa Dias is a lovely tiled restaurant that features models of Porto's

3+ ARTE, a café, gallery and shop hybrid

bridges on its walls. The main reason to visit, though, is for substantial portions of good-value food. Dishes of pork, grilled chicken or steak come with mountains of chips, or you can choose the fresh fish of the day. €€

De Castro

MAP PAGE 62, POCKET MAP E9
Gaia Espaço Porto Cruz, Largo Miguel Bombarda 23 Ⓦ myportocruz.com.
On the third floor of the modern Espaço Porto Cruz building, this restaurant serves sandwiches, salads and tapas at lunchtime, plus more substantial dishes in the evening, such as veal cheek and creamy rice with *choriço* – all accompanied by serene river views. €€

Dourum

MAP PAGE 62, POCKET MAP F8
Av Diogo Leite 454 Ⓣ 220 917 911.
This tiny, traditional restaurant has a smattering of tables that spills onto the street outside and boasts great views of the river. Come here for the tasty tapas, such as octopus

salad and sautéed squid, or opt for a hearty main course, perhaps grilled pork fillet or *bacalhau à bras*. €€

Taberninha do Manel

MAP PAGE 62, POCKET MAP E9
Av Diogo Leite 308
Ⓦ taberninhadomanel.com.
Long-established traditional restaurant whose tables outside on the waterfront offer great views of Porto across the river. It serves reasonably priced *petiscos*, such as hot roast pork sandwiches and a tasty wild mushroom and bean stew, as well as more substantial dishes and, of course, the mighty *francesinhas*. €€€

Toca do Coelho

MAP PAGE 62, POCKET MAP D9
Largo Sampaio Bruno 2 Ⓣ 223 754 820.
At the side of the market building, with seats on a cobbled side street, this tiny local restaurant rustles up good-value lunches. Pork, chicken and deliciously fresh *pescada*; there are good salads, too. €€

Vinum

MAP PAGE 62

Graham's, Rua do Agro 141

Ⓦ vinumatgrahams.com.

This spacious restaurant sits at the front of the vast Graham's port lodge, with a terrace that offers far-reaching views over town. The service is sleek and the food excellent: expect the likes of squid rice cooked in its own ink or suckling pig with truffles, and, of course, you'll be offered a Graham's port at the end of the meal. Reservations advised. €€€€

The Yeatman

MAP PAGE 62

Rua do Choupelo

Ⓦ the-yeatman-hotel.com.

With two Michelin Stars to its name, *The Yeatman*'s gourmet restaurant can lay claim to being the top dining room in Portugal. You'll be served by a fleet of waiters who are every bit as impressive as the views over town. You can get the full tasting menu for a whopping €250; dishes use largely local produce – sea urchins, turbot or swordfish with kumquats, followed by sublime desserts such

as chocolate tripe. Each dish is accompanied by one of the restaurant's eighty varieties of wine or port (around €125 extra). €€€€

Port tastings

Kopke House

MAP PAGE 62, POCKET MAP E9

Av Diogo Leite 312 Ⓦ kopke1638.com.

The three-storey *Kopke House*, right on the riverside, specializes in port and chocolate pairing. Made in Porto by Arcádia since the 1930s, the chocolates have been specifically selected to complement the wines. Also offers organic olive oil tastings.

Quevedo Cellar

MAP PAGE 62

Rua de Santa Marinha 11

Ⓦ quevedoportwine.com.

This small family-run port and wine producer has a relaxed tasting room, tucked away behind the main riverfront street, with a wood burner and a piano. Here, you can sample individual glasses of port or wine from the family's vineyards along the Douro.

Vinum, at the fore of Graham's

Terrace Lounge 360

Sogevinus

MAP PAGE 62, POCKET MAP C9
Av Ramos Pinto 280 Ⓦ sogevinus.com.
Right on the riverfront, the
Sogevinus shop has a great
selection of ports from its own
brands, including Burmester,
Cálem, Kopke, Barros and
Gilberts. Individual tastings
available, or you can sample a
selection of five ports, including a
choice of vintage ports.

Bars and nightlife

Caves Cálem

MAP PAGE 62, POCKET MAP E9
Av Diogo Leite 344
Ⓦ fadoinporto.com. Charge.
The Cálem port lodge puts on
atmospheric fado concerts in its
cellars, with Portuguese guitar and
singers. Concerts also include a
tour and port tasting.

Dick's Bar

MAP PAGE 62
The Yeatman, Rua do Choupelo
Ⓣ 220 133 100.
Much less formal than *The
Yeatman's* restaurant (see page

70), *Dick's Bar* is a great place
to treat yourself to a drink. You
can choose from no fewer than
25,000 bottles of wine, not to
mention a variety of port-based
cocktails – try the punchy mix
of Grand Marnier, orange zest
and mint leaves. The smart decor
features big comfy sofas and glass
tabletops crammed with corks;
there's also live music (usually
Thurs–Sat). However, the big
draw here is the staggering view of
Porto: settle down on the outside
terrace, on a sofa, or by the fire
pit, and watch the sun set over
the city.

Terrace Lounge 360

MAP PAGE 62, POCKET MAP E9
Espaço Porto Cruz, Largo Miguel Bombarda
23 Ⓣ 220 092 5340.
Head up to the top floor of the
Espaço Porto Cruz complex to
knock back a glass or two of port
at this breeze-cooled open-air
rooftop bar with great views –
sunset is the best time to come as
you can watch the lights slowly
coming on over the river and city
opposite. Also serves a small menu
of light bites and lunches.

Miragaia and Massarelos

West of the centre lie the appealing districts of Miragaia and Massarelos, many of whose streets tumble down steep slopes that line the River Douro. On Miragaia's earthy riverfront, the Museu dos Transportes e Comunicações, housed in the city's huge former customs house, is the highlight of a cluster of engaging museums. Steeply uphill lies the extensive gardens of the Palácio de Cristal, a tranquil spot to while away an afternoon. Sharing the garden's stunning views over the Douro, the adjacent Museu Romântico da Quinta da Macierihna gives an insight into how Porto's wealthy port merchants once lived. Heading back into town, the Museu Nacional Soares dos Reis is one of Portugal's finest art museums.

Museu dos Transportes e Comunicações

MAP PAGE 74, POCKET MAP B6
Rua Nova de Alfândega ⓦamtc.pt. Charge; access to the ground floor of the customs house is free. Tram #1 from Infante, or bus #500 from São Bento.

The Neoclassical Alfândega, or customs house, was built on a former fishermen's beach between 1860 and 1880. It's a vast building that was originally designed to store the cargo of up to forty ships, but was imaginatively renovated

Museu dos Transportes e Comunicações in the Neoclassical Alfândega

Porto's tram routes

Porto has three remaining **tram routes**, all of which are great fun to travel on. Tram #22 and #18 leave from the top of the Jardim da Cordoaria; #22 takes a circular route through the city centre via Torre dos Clérigos, Batalha and back via Aliados and the Igreja do Carmo, while #18 heads southwest to Massarelos, ending up by the Museu do Carro Eléctrico. If you only have time for one trip, choose tram #1. Starting from the end of Rua de Alfândega, it trundles alongside the river on a scenic 25- minute ride to Foz do Douro. Note that Andante passes are not valid on the trams (except for monthly passes); for details of tickets see Essentials (see page 124).

in the late twentieth century by famous Porto architect Eduardo Souto de Moura and now houses the **Museu dos Transportes e Comunicações** (Transport and Communications Museum). You can look round the ground floor of the huge customs house with its grand public rooms and access to the riverbank behind for free, while the upper two floors house the museum and its various exhibitions. On the first floor, the imaginative **Communications museum** looks at how trade, TV and radio have helped communications with the rest of the world, with plenty of interactive displays that children will enjoy including a giant megaphone, some very bulky early computers, TVs and record players. In the western wing of the first floor, the **Engine of the Republic** exhibition displays some of the cars used by Portugal's presidents since the birth of the republic in 1910, from the early horse-drawn carriages to the armoured Mercedes favoured by former dictator Salazar and the Rolls Royce Phantom III bought for England's Queen Elizabeth II's state visit in 1957. Look out for the distinctive POR numberplate that all the president's official cars carry. You can also view entertaining authentic news footage of the cars being used on state occasions. Although the captions are only in Portuguese for this exhibition, you can pick up an English-language guide at the desk.

World of Discoveries

MAP PAGE 74, POCKET MAP B6
Rua de Miragaia 106 Ⓦ worldofdiscoveries. com. Charge. Tram #1 from Infante, or bus #500 from São Bento.

This informative **museum** has interactive displays themed around the famous Portuguese explorers of the fifteenth and sixteenth centuries, such as Ferdinand Magellan, Vasco da Gama, Bartolomeu Dias and Henry the Navigator. Actors re-enact scenes of the swash-buckling explorers in replicas of the newly 'discovered' lands. You can also explore a recreated shipyard to learn about the vessels and life on board the ships. The highlight of the museum, however, is an entertaining boat trip down an internal river, through tableaux of the foreign lands 'discovered' by the Portuguese, including Africa, India, Japan, Brazil and Macao.

Igreja de São Pedro de Miragaia

MAP PAGE 74, POCKET MAP B6
Largo de São Pedro de Miragaia. Free. Tram #1 from Infante, or bus #500 from São Bento.

Tucked away off Rua Miragaia, the beautiful blue-tiled Igreja de **São Pedro de Miragaia** was built in the 1830s on the site of a medieval

The World of Discoveries is dedicated to the famous Portuguese explorers

Porto Planetarium

VIA PANORÂMICA

VIA PANORÂMICA EDGAR CARDOSO

RUA DA PENA

RUA DE DOM PEDRO V

RUA DO

RUA CAP. SALGUEIRO MAIA

RUA DA B.C.ª VIAGEM

RUA DA B.C.ª VIAGEM

RUA ARCEDIAGO VAN ZELLER

RUA ABADE DE

CALÇ. DA ARRÁBIDA

& 5 (450m)

Ponte da Arrábida (250m)

RUA DO BICALHO

BICALHO   RUA DO OURO

RUA DL BOA VISTA

Museu do
Carro
Eléctrico

Museu Romântico
da Quinta da
Macierinha

N

ALAMEDA

MUSEU DO CARRO ELÉCTRICO (T)

6

RUA FONTE DE MASS.

RUA OLIVEIRA

RUA CANDO MADUREIRA

TRAV. DA MACIEIRINHA

O QUINTO

IGREJA DE
MASSARELOS

TRAV. DE
ENTRE QUINTAS

(H)   BASÍLIO TELES

18

RUA DA RESTAURAÇÃO

L'GO DO
OURO

R. DO CRISTELO

RUA DO CAIS
DAS PEDRAS

7

ENTRE
QUINTAS

CAIS DAS
PEDRAS

VIADUTO DO CAIS DAS PEDRAS

CAFÉS

Pimenta Rosa	2
Quintal Bioshop	1
Rota do Chá	4

RESTAURANTS

Antiqvvm	6
Bugo	3
Casa d'Oro	5
Papavinhos	8
Taberna do Barqueiro	9
Taberna do Cais das Pedras	7

SHOPS

Bombarda 498	4
Ó! Galería	2
Scar.ID	1
Tendinha dos Acessórios	3

ACCOMMODATION

Eurostar das Artes	2
Pensão Favorita	4
Porta Azul	5
Porto Gallery Hostel	3
Rosa et al Townhouse	1
Vincci Porto	6

BAR

| Catraio | 1 |

| 0 | metres | 250 |
| 0 | yards | 250 |

CAIS DO CAVACO

Miragaia and Massarelos

Inaugurações Simultâneas

Rua Miguel Bombarda and the streets around it are at their liveliest during the **Inaugurações Simultâneas** (literally, simultaneous openings), when many of the area's art galleries launch new shows, exhibitions and artists on the same day. The shops stay open in the evening and there's music, entertainment and performance art on the streets, which fill with art buffs, hipsters and the general public checking out the culture and events. They take place six times a year on a Saturday, starting at 4pm: check with the tourist board for the exact dates.

church, which was one of the oldest in Porto. Inside, check out the ornate Rococo wooden and gilt carvings, as well as the impressive sixteenth-century Flemish Pentecost triptych.

Museu do Carro Eléctrico

MAP PAGE 74, POCKET MAP A10
Alameda Basílio Teles 51
Ⓦmuseudocarroelectrico.pt. Charge.
Tram #1 from Infante, or bus #500 from São Bento.

Porto's trams #1 and #18 make a fitting halt on the riverside outside the **Museu do Carro Eléctrico** (Tram Museum). In the echoing spaces of a former power station, you can admire Iberia's oldest streetcar (1872) alongside lots of other gleaming vintage specimens, many made by companies in Birkenhead or Preston in England which gave the trams the nickname "English Cars". Look out for the Vagoneta 80, used to carry fresh

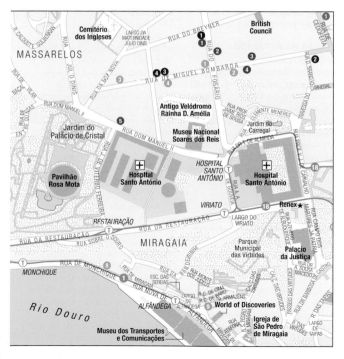

Ponte da Arrábida

fish from the market in Matosinhos to Porto's central markets in the 1930s. Black-and-white photos also give an insight into the importance public transport has had in the development of the city.

Ponte da Arrábida

MAP PAGE 74
Porto Bridge Climb: Rua d'Ouro 680 Ⓦ portobridgeclimb.com. Charge. Tram #1 from Infante, or bus #500 from São Bento.

Designed in 1963 by experimental engineer Edgar Cardoso, the arched **Pont da Arrábida** carries the busy A1 from Porto's Campo Alegre to the district of Arrábida. When it opened, it had the longest reinforced concrete bridge span in the world, at 270m. There's a small exhibition space at the foot of the bridge showing you how it was built. More exciting, however, is to climb the bridge with Porto Bridge Climb.

The ascent involves a slow, steady and somewhat hairy climb up steps to the top of the 70m-high central concrete arch. The view from the top is amazing, but make sure you wear sensible shoes and avoid wearing skirts or dresses, which can interfere with the harness.

Jardim do Palácio de Cristal

MAP PAGE 74, POCKET MAP A4
Rua Dom Manuel II Ⓣ 225 320 080. Free. Bus #200 from Aliados.

The attractive, landscaped **Jardim do Palácio de Cristal** is designed around the centrepiece Pavilhão Rosa Mota, which was named after Porto's best-known athlete and Olympic marathon runner. Resembling a kind of concrete tea cosy, the current pavilion was built in the 1950s to replace a far more elegant 1860s iron-and-glass "Crystal Palace". However, the real draw here is the surrounding **gardens** that tumble down a steep hill and are dotted with areas of woodland. The gardens spread out over a series of terraces frequented by strutting peacocks. There's an avenue of lime trees and stunning river views towards the Ponte da Arrábida and, beyond, Foz from high vantage points on the south side. The municipal library is located near the main entrance, and a cluster of other buildings and galleries here put on exhibitions, workshops, summer concerts and children's activities. There's also a little kiosk café situated by the lake.

Museu Romântico da Quinta da Macieirinha

MAP PAGE 74, POCKET MAP C10
Rua de Entre Quintas 220. Charge.
Bus #200 from Aliados.

Originally built for a merchant's family in the nineteenth century, the **Quinta da Macieirinha** was bought by port wine millionaire Antonio Ferreira Pinto Basto, who used it as a summer house. He hosted a variety of illustrous guests here, including the King of Piedmont and Sardinia who stayed after his exile, and died here in 1849. The house has been renovated and refurnished with genuine furniture and artefacts from the period, giving a fascinating insight into life among Porto's wealthy nineteenth-century society. There's a billiard room, ballroom and private chapel and, as ever, the grounds are a beautiful, peaceful oasis with great views over the Douro.

Museu Nacional Soares dos Reis

MAP PAGE 74, POCKET MAP B4
Rua Dom Manuel II 44

Ⓦ museusoaresdosreis.gov.pt. Charge, free on 1st Sun of the month until 2pm.

A five-minute walk from the Jardim da Cordoaria, behind the hospital, stands the **Museu Nacional Soares dos Reis**. The oldest art museum in Portugal, it was founded in 1833 to preserve works confiscated from dissolved monasteries and convents. The present building, into which the collection was moved in the 1940s, was once a royal residence that served as the French headquarters in the Peninsular War.

The museum takes its name from sculptor **António Soares dos Reis** (1847–89), whose best-known work, *O Desterrado* (The Exile), is here, along with an extensive display of Portuguese art from the sixteenth to twentieth centuries. But it's the applied and decorative art that's perhaps most engaging – the museum contains excellent collections of gold jewellery, religious silverwork, Portuguese glassware, earthenware and textiles, delicate Chinese ceramics, noble French furniture and painted screens and lacquered

Jardim do Palácio de Cristal offers fine views towards the Ponte da Arrábida

Michelin-starred cuisine and the importance of grandmas

In recent years, the Porto area has become a **culinary hotbed** with several Michelin-starred chefs flying the flag for regional ingredients. Ricardo Costa's creative take on traditional cuisine has brought two Michelin Stars to *The Yeatman* (see page 70), using cooking skills passed down from his grandmother. With one Michelin star, Vítor Matos also uses regional produce in the splendidly ornate *Antiqvvm* (see page 80). Out near the seafront, Pedro Lemos also claims to have taken inspiration from his grandmother who sold fish at the market in Matosinhos: unsurprisingly, the menu at his eponymous Michelin-starred restaurant (see page 98) is excellent for fish and seafood dishes. Just north of Porto, at the wonderful seafront *Casa de Chá da Boa Nova* (see page 97), Porto-born Rui Paula reinterprets recipes used by – you guessed it – his grandmother, and has garnered two Michelin stars for it. While all these restaurants are undoubtedly pricey, they are less expensive than UK equivalents – and all are worth splashing out on. If they are still beyond your budget, head to the Porto outpost of Lisbon-based, Michelin-star chef José Avillez: here, in the heart of Porto, the *Cantinho do Avillez* bistro (see page 56) serves up interesting and innovative contemporary Portuguese food at affordable prices.

cabinets from the Far East. Special exhibitions concentrate on particular periods, artists or themes, and you could spend hours just browsing; there's also a (rather unkempt, but pretty) garden and a café, which serves a good-value daily lunch.

Rua Miguel Bombarda

The formerly rundown street of **Rua Miguel Bombarda** has transformed itself into the centre of Porto's artistic quarter. The city's cultural renaissance took root when a scattering of independent art galleries sprang up along the street during the depths of the economic crisis. The creative enclave is a good place to browse, filled with contemporary art galleries, workshops, cool concept stores, vintage shops, design boutiques, cafés and tearooms, though you won't find anything open much before noon, or on a Sunday. Some of the

street's more interesting galleries include the **Cruzes Canhoto** at no. 452 (Ⓦ cruzescanhoto. com), where you can buy brightly painted models and primitive and folk art; the upmarket **São Mamede** gallery at no. 624 (Ⓦ saomamede.com), which sells sculptures by the likes of Victor Ribeiro for a hefty price tag; and the more accessible **Ó! Galería**, at no. 61 (Ⓦ ogaleria.com), with changing exhibitions of paintings and sketches by artists such as Joanna Pinto, and a good range of more accessibly priced prints and illustrations for sale. The street is also home to the **Centro Comercial Bombarda**, at no. 285, where you can find a range of quirky independent shops selling everything from vintage clothing, toys, home-made jewellery and crafts to art, books, posters and vinyl. There are also food shops and a café, plus a grassy courtyard to chill out in.

Shops

Bombarda 498

MAP PAGE 74, POCKET MAP A3
Rua Miguel Bombarda 498 ☎ 223 229 634.
Designer boutique selling
reasonably priced bags and clothes
plus trendy brands such as Tanya
Heath shoes, with their signature
detachable heels that come in
different styles and heights, and A
Favela do Biquini, with its skimpy
Brazilian swimwear.

Ó! Galería

MAP PAGE 74, POCKET MAP C3
Rua Miguel Bombarda 61 ☉ ogaleria.com.
Hundreds of humorous
illustrations line the walls at this
dinky gallery, jostling for space
with framed prints. Tables are piled
with cool postcards, notebooks and
other covetable gems.

Scar.ID

MAP PAGE 74, POCKET MAP B3
Rua do Rosário 253 ☉ scar-id.com.
Trendy shop/gallery selling jewellery,
ceramics, furniture and clothing
by up-and-coming Portuguese
designers. It's not cheap, but there
are some interesting and unusual

pieces here – and you may pick up a
bargain from the next big name.

Tendinha dos Acessórios

MAP PAGE 74, POCKET MAP A3
Rua Miguel Bombarda 468 ☎ 935 015 271.
Women's clothes made by local
designers at reasonable prices, as well
as a few preloved and vintage items.
Also sells soaps by Viseu company,
Só Sabão, made from local, natural
ingredients. There's another branch
in Foz, at Rua de Gondarém 247.

Cafés

Pimenta Rosa

MAP PAGE 74, POCKET MAP B3
Loja 14, CC Bombarda, 285 Rua Miguel
Bombarda ☎ 933 662 289.
Inside the CC Bombarda shopping
mall, this canteen-style restaurant
serves excellent-value buffet meals,
such as salads, quiche, meat dishes,
fish or pizza. The cakes are great too
– particularly the chocolate ones. €

Quintal Bioshop

MAP PAGE 74, POCKET MAP B3
Rua do Rosario 177 ☎ 222 010 008.
Lovely little health food shop
meets vegetarian café, selling

Scar.ID showcases the work of Portuguese designers

a variety of organic and eco-friendly food and fresh, seasonal produce. The café at the back dishes up veggie and vegan food, including soups, tofu sandwiches, beanburgers and juices, and there's also a pretty garden. €

Rota do Chá

MAP PAGE 74, POCKET MAP A3
Rua Miguel Bombarda 457
Ⓦ rotadocha.com.

Tucked behind a shop that sells a variety of loose leaf teas, plus colourful tins and caddies of exotic brews, is a hideaway tearoom in a pretty Eastern-inspired garden, dotted with giant buddhas, low tables with tree-shaded seats and breeze-cooled arbours. It's a great place for a lazy afternoon with a good book, a big pot of fancy leaves and a *tosta*, or the dish of the day, such as prawn rice. €

Restaurants

Antiqvvm

MAP PAGE 74, POCKET MAP C10
Rua de Entre Quintas 220 Ⓦ antiqvvm.pt.
Beautifully positioned in a corner of the Jardim do Palácio de Cristal, with its own little garden offering stunning Douro views, this is one of Porto's most alluring restaurants.

Chef Vítor Matos (see page 78) has deservedly earned the nineteenth-century former *quinta* a Michelin star. You can choose from the tasting menu or go à la carte (though both are at least €120). Expect the likes of scallop and champagne ravioli, mussels escabeche, or black pork with Douro red wine sauce, all with top Portuguese wines. €€€€

Bugo

MAP PAGE 74, POCKET MAP A3
Rua Miguel Bombarda 598
Ⓦ bugoartburgers.eatbu.com.
Seriously good burgers, made from free-range meat sourced by Portuguese farmers. You can choose from chicken, beef, tuna, sausage or chickpea burgers, and then add a variety of gourmet-style toppings, including goat's cheese; pineapple and bacon; port, prosciutto and cheese; or sautéed turnip greens and chestnut sauce. The burgers come with a heap of chips – if you choose not to have the bun, you get extra rice or roasted potatoes as well as chips. €€

Casa d'Oro

MAP PAGE 74
Rua Ouro 797 ☎ 226 106 012.
This excellent Italian restaurant and pizzeria couldn't get much closer to the river, with a superb outdoor

The tranquil garden at *Rota do Chá*

The riverside *Casa d'Oro*

terrace facing the Ponte de Arrábida – indeed, the engineers were housed in the building when they constructed it. Authentic Italian cuisine features the likes of *ossobuco alla Milanese* (veal with a vegetable and wine sauce) and a range of pasta and pizzas, not to mention desserts including a sumptuous tiramisu. €€€

Papavinhos

MAP PAGE 74, POCKET MAP A6 & D11
Rua de Monchique 23
W papavinhos.eatbu.com.
Just up from the Museu dos Transportes e Comunicações and on the route of tram #1, this contemporary restaurant is on two floors, with fine river views from the top one. The innovative menu features the likes of spicy clams, mussels and a long list of fresh fish and meat, together with a fine and filling *arroz de marisco*. €€€

Taberna do Barqueiro

MAP PAGE 74, POCKET MAP B6
Rua de Miragaia 123–124 ☎ 937 691 732.
A small, friendly local tavern with tables out on the pretty square opposite the Museu dos Transportes e Comunicações. It's an alluring spot for a glass or two of Douro red wine and a range of tapas (*pataniscas*, *alheira*, hams and local cheeses). It also serves tasty

mains (grilled meat or fish of the day). The interior is cosy but small, so it's best to reserve. €€€

Taberna do Cais das Pedras

MAP PAGE 74, POCKET MAP C11
Rua de Monchique 65–68 ☎ 913 164 584.
In a lovely tiled building with a solitary palm tree at the front, this local restaurant serves traditional Porto cuisine in very reasonably sized tapas-style portions – dishes include octopus, clams, *choriço* and snails. *Azulejos* adorn the cosy interior, and there's an outdoor dining terrace overlooking the river. Wine comes in handmade ceramic jugs. €€€

Bar

Catraio

MAP PAGE 74, POCKET MAP C3
Rua de Cedofeita 256 ☎ 934 360 070.
Part bar and part shop, *Catraio* specializes in craft beers from microbreweries around Portugal and beyond. If you thought Portuguese beer consisted of only Super Bock and Sagres, think again: here, you can sample stouts, amber ales and many others, with the week's specials chalked up on a board. The Sovina chestnutty brown ale is a good one to start with.

Boavista and the west

The highlight of the well-to-do suburb of Boavista is the Casa da Música, Porto's main cultural centre and its most stunning chunk of modern architecture. Equally impressive are Iberia's largest synagogue, the Sinagoge Kadoorie, and the expansive magnolia-lined Cemitério de Agramonte. It's a short ride west to the leafy Jardim Botânico do Porto, while there are further architectural attractions in the form of the Fundação Serralves, where buildings house contemporary art exhibitions in extensive grounds. The area's other attractions include the lively Bom Sucesso market, one of Portugal's oldest churches, Igreja de São Martinho de Cedofeita, and Boavista FC, the city's second football club.

Jardim Botânico do Porto

MAP PAGE 84
Rua do Campo Alegre 1191
Ⓦ jardimbotanico.up.pt. Free.
Bus #200 from Aliados.

Part of the University of Porto, the attractive **botanical gardens** were laid out in 1951. The gardens are an appealing mixture of the formal and the wild, with steps and paths leading up through plants from different habitats. Topiary, rose gardens and the most formal gardens are centred around the elegant **Casa Andresen**, named after the owners of the estate before it was given to the state. Beyond here there's an arid zone, with various cacti and succulents as well as greenhouses with larger cacti and beautiful orchids. Then, further down the hill you'll find a lake and mature trees, including magnolias that are magnificent in early spring.

Synagogue Kadoorie

MAP PAGE 84
Rua de Guerra Junqueiro 340
Ⓣ 911 768 596. Charge for guided tours (by appointment only). Ⓜ Casa da Música.

Despite Portugal being an overwhelmingly Catholic country, Porto is home to Iberia's largest synagogue, the **Synagogue Kadoorie** with its impressive Art Deco facade. It was founded largely due to the efforts of Captain Barros Basto, a World War I veteran, who was surprised to discover his heritage when his grandfather confessed to being Jewish on his deathbed in the 1920s. During the sixteenth-century inquisitions, Jews had been forced to convert to New Christians and open worship was difficult until the twentieth century. So, Barros Basto began a campaign to reconvert New Christians back to the Jewish faith, travelling round Portugal by donkey to do so; he also taught himself Hebrew and set up a Jewish newspaper, *Halapid*. With the support of prominent Jews around Europe (including Baron de Rothschild of Paris), he raised the funds to build "the cathedral of the north". The Kadoorie opened in 1938, the same year that other synagogues were being ransacked by Nazi Germany. A small museum explores the history of the Kadoorie.

Cemitério de Agramonte

MAP PAGE 84
Rua de Agramonte
Ⓣ 226 066 604. Free. Ⓜ Casa da Música.

Built in 1855 in response to a cholera epidemic, the **Cemitério**

de Agramonte was a simple burial ground until the 1870s when elaborate mausoleums began to be built. These became ever more extravagant as the cemetery became the resting place of choice for Porto's wealthy, as well as for writers, artists and musicians, including painter António Carneiro, violinist Guillermina Suggia, photographer Emílio Biel and architect Tomás Soller. It's a tranquil and interesting place to explore: stroll along the magnolia-lined paths and admire the enormous, ornate mausoleums, some boasting sculptures by the likes of Soares dos Reis, António Teixeira Lopes and Alves Pinto.

Also, peer into the impressive, if rather eerie, oval-shaped Jazigo Municipal (the municipal burial building), built in granite and iron, where the city's poorer citizens were buried stacked on shelves.

Mercado do Bom Sucesso

MAP PAGE 84
Praça Bom Sucesso 3
Ⓦ mercadobomsucesso.pt. Daily
8am–11pm. Ⓜ Casa da Música.
Originally built in the 1950s as a fresh produce market, the renovated **Mercado do Bom Sucesso** now houses food stalls, boutique shops, small cafés and local bars, plus a small section selling fresh fruit and vegetables – there's even a hotel (see page 117). The impressive, hangar-like structure is big enough to park a plane or two.

It's a great place for lunch, with everything from pizza and vegetarian food to seafood and sushi on the menu – the stall with the longest lunchtime queue is *Leitão do Zé*, which sells rolls filled with spit-roasted suckling pig and chips for bargain prices. There's entertainment in the evenings, with the likes of live music, DJs and workshops.

Rotunda da Boavista

The northwestern edge of the city centre – 2km from downtown Aliados – is marked by the large park-cum-roundabout, which is called the Praça Mouzinho de Albuquerque, but is more commonly known as the **Rotunda da Boavista**. The mighty obelisk in the centre commemorates the defeat of the French in the Peninsular War

Cemitério de Agramonte

Boavista and the west

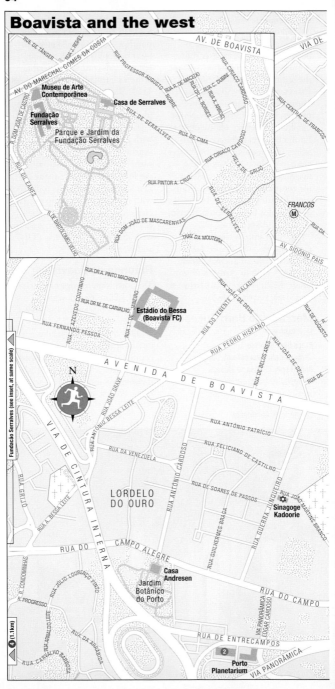

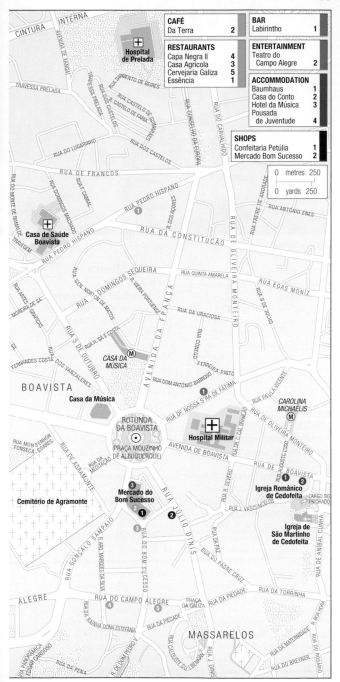

CAFÉ		BAR	
Da Terra	2	Labirintho	1

RESTAURANTS		ENTERTAINMENT	
Capa Negra II	4	Teatro do	
Casa Agricola	3	Campo Alegre	2
Cervejaria Galiza	5		
Essência	1	

ACCOMMODATION
Baumhaus — 1
Casa do Conto — 2
Hotel da Música — 3
Pousada
de Juventude — 4

SHOPS
Confeitaria Petúlia — 1
Mercado Bom Sucesso — 2

0 metres 250
0 yards 250

Fundação Serralves

(1808–14), with a Portuguese lion squatting on top of a vanquished French eagle.

Despite the swirling traffic, the rotunda is a pleasant place to rest from the heat under the trees. It also marks the start of Porto's longest road, the 5km-long Avenida da Boavista, which runs all the way out to the coast at Foz do Douro.

Igreja de São Martinho de Cedofeita

MAP PAGE 84, POCKET MAP B1
Largo do Priorado, off Rua Aníbal Cunha
☎ 222 000 635. Free.
Ⓜ Lapa or Ⓜ Carolina Michaelis.
Located a few blocks off the Rotunda is the very simple **Igreja de São Martinho de Cedofeita**, which some claim has its origins as far back as the ninth century AD – making it one of the oldest churches in Iberia. However, the existing Romanesque building is a thirteenth-century remodelling of a church whose existence can only be dated with certainty to 1087. Whatever its origins, Cedofeita is unique in being Portugal's only Romanesque church to have kept its original dome, which is supported by bulky exterior buttresses.

Casa da Música

MAP PAGE 84
Av da Boavista 604–610 Ⓦ casadamusica. com. Charge for tours. Charge, though some events are free. Ⓜ Casa da Música.
Rem Koolhaas' superb modern cultural centre, the **Casa da Música** – a vast white wedge on a bare esplanade – looks as if the Mothership has landed, an impression reinforced by the steel staircase leading up into the black mouth of the entrance. It's a striking building with undulating ground outside where BMX riders cycle, and walls that jut out at angles above your head. Porto's major concert hall, it opened to great fanfare in 2005 and now has an international reputation, not just for recitals and classical concerts – it's home of the Orquestra Nacional do Porto, one of the country's leading symphony orchestras – but for early and contemporary music, fado, world, jazz, folk and experimental music too. Attending a concert or event is the best way to see the building, especially inside the 1300-seat Grand Auditorium with its glass walls, but there are daily, hour-long guided visits if you want to know more about its dramatic design

The other Porto football team

Less well known than its city rivals Porto, **Boavista** in fact has an impressive pedigree. Founded in 1903, the club has won five Portuguese Cups and one Championship in 2001, making them only the second Portuguese team to ever win it outside the top teams of Porto, Sporting and Benfica. The 2004 construction of the impressive Estádio do Bessa for the European Championships proved to be the start of a rocky time for the club. Steeped in debt, Boavista was then found guilty of bribery and relegated to the second tier in 2008. It was not until 2014 that the club had sufficient funds to be allowed back into the top division.

and construction. There's also an impressive black-and-white tiled roof terrace, top-floor restaurant and excellent ground floor café that serves sandwiches and pastries.

Estádio do Bessa

MAP PAGE 84

Rua 1 de Janeiro, off Av da Boavista ⓦ boavistafc.pt. Bus #201 from Av dos Aliados, or ⓜ Francos, which is 1km northeast of the stadium.

The modern and compact **Estádio do Bessa Século XXI** is home to Boavista, Porto's second football team. The 28,200-seat stadium was built for the 2004 European Championship, but the club rarely gets anything like that number of spectators, so it is fairly easy to get tickets for matches, even against the big boys such as Sporting or Benfica. It's a homely ground, and if you want to find out more about the club or the other sports that it runs (including boxing, volleyball and handball), there is a small museum at the stadium, but this is only open on request. Tickets can be bought on the day at the stadium or via ⓦboavistafc.pt.

Fundação Serralves

MAP PAGE 84

Rua Dom João de Castro 210 ⓦ serralves. pt. Charge; both free first Sun of the month 10am–1pm. ⓜ Casa da Música, or bus #502 from Bolhão or bus #203 from Rotunda da Boavista.

If there's one must-see cultural attraction in Porto, it's the contemporary art museum and park run by the Fundação Serralves, 4km west of the centre. The **Museu de Arte Contemporânea** is the work of Porto architect Álvaro Siza Vieira, and is a minimalist triumph of white facades and terraces strikingly set in an overwhelmingly green park. The museum holds 4300 artworks from the 1960s to the present day, though there is no permanent collection: instead, several changing exhibitions a year draw on the works of Portuguese and international artists, such as Joan Miró. Other exhibitions are held in the separate, pink Art Deco **Casa de Serralves** in the grounds.

You can get an idea of the main building from the outside, and from the terrace café, the more formal restaurant and the museum shop (all free to enter). And if the exhibitions aren't to your taste, you miss nothing by just visiting the expansive, surrounding **park**. Indeed, many people prefer this to the museum itself, and it's easy to spend a lazy afternoon here, winding along swept gravel paths and clipped lawns before descending wooded tracks to the herb gardens and farmland beyond, grazed by goats and cattle.

There are art installations dotted around and a teahouse in a glade with a vine colonnade. July and August see a sequence of "Jazz no Parque" (Jazz in the Park) **concerts** held in the gardens.

Shop

Confeitaria Petúlia

MAP PAGE 84
Rua de Júlio Dinis 775 ⓦ petulia.pt.
Confeitaria Petúlia is the place to go if you're looking to satiate a sugar craving. Experienced pastry chefs use only the best ingredients to whip up a tantalizing array of sweet treats, such as *pão-de-ló*, a light sponge cake often eaten at Easter, and *bolo-rei*, a fruit cake enjoyed as part of Christmas festivities. More suitcase-friendly options include *bolinhos de coco* (coconut cookies) and *húngaros* (chocolate-dipped biscuits). Or pick up an oven-warm pie or meat croquette to go.

Café

Da Terra

MAP PAGE 84
Mercado do Bom Sucesso,
Praça Bom Sucesso 3.
Vegetarians should seek out the tiny *Da Terra*, tucked away in the far corner of the Bom Sucesso market – there's a daily selection of freshly prepared salads and tasty hot dishes, such as ratatouille, bean burgers and soya fillet in asparagus sauce. It also serves up lovely cakes and fresh juices. €€

Restaurants

Capa Negra II

MAP PAGE 84
Rua do Campo Alegre 191
ⓦ capanegra.com.
A metal brewing still marks the entrance to this modern and extremely popular *cervejaria* – expect queues at the weekend – which serves food until late. It champions its *francesinhas* but the steaks and shellfish are just as good; portions are huge. €€€

Casa Agricola

MAP PAGE 84
Rua Bom Sucesso 241
ⓦ casaagricola.eatbu.com.
Cosy café-restaurant in an atmospheric eighteenth-century former merchant's house – all dark wood and chandeliers. A broad menu features the likes of monkfish rice with prawns and grilled octopus, black pork and duck risotto. €€€

Da Terra, a vegetarian-friendly spot

Capa Negra II, a champion of the belt-loosening *francesinhas*

Cervejaria Galiza

MAP PAGE 84

Rua do Campo Alegre 55 ☎ 222 448 213.
This modern *cervejaria* serves up a meat- and seafood-leaning menu until the early hours. Expect the likes of pork chops, hake fillets and a filling *arroz de marisco*. €€€

Essência

MAP PAGE 84

Rua de Pedro Hispano 1190
Ⓦ essenciavegetariano.pt.
Light and airy haunt dishing up delicious vegetarian food, from home-made soups and colourful salads to creative dishes like pineapple carpaccio drizzled with mint pesto and served with caramelized cherries. Also offers meat dishes such as *feijoada* (pork and bean stew). The outdoor terrace is a romantic spot. €€€

Mercado Bom Sucesso

MAP PAGE 84

Praça do Bom Sucesso 74–90
Ⓦ mercadobomsucesso.pt.
You'll find many a local at Mercado Bom Sucesso lingering over a glass of wine and plate of cheese and ham after a day's work. A cluster of food stalls and restaurants awaits hungry patrons, including traditional Portuguese plates at *Maria's Tasca*, succulent roast meats at *Salt & Pepper*, fresh seafood dishes at *Mariscaria* and tasty poké bowls at *My'Kai*. €€€

Bar

Labirintho

MAP PAGE 84

Rua Nossa Senhora de Fátima 334
Ⓦ Casa da Música.
Great bar set in a quirky converted house with a shaded back garden. It also functions as a gallery space and bookshop, with occasional live music, and attracts an arty crowd.

Entertainment

Teatro do Campo Alegre

MAP PAGE 84

Rua das Estrelas Ⓦ teatromunicipaldo
porto.pt. Bus #200 from Aliados.
An innovative playhouse putting on a vibrant blend of music, theatre, cinema, animation and public lectures.

Foz do Douro, Matosinhos and Leça da Palmeira

Where the River Douro meets the Atlantic Ocean, Foz do Douro makes an excellent day-trip from Porto – or you could even base yourself here and explore the city by tram. Formerly a fishing port, it's now an affluent suburb with some pleasant sandy beaches, where locals enjoy cold swims in summer and blowy walks between its two sea forts in winter. It's also home to Porto's largest green space, the Parque de Cidade, and the enjoyable Sea Life aquarium. Neighbouring Matosinhos, its large beach aside, has a far more industrial skyline than Foz do Douro. Despite its unappealing appearance, the city has undergone something of a renaissance, with its own metro line connecting it to Porto and a swanky cruise terminal. The main draw here, though, is to visit one of its famed fish restaurants. Further north up the coast, the industrial town of Leça da Palmeira has a broad town beach for surfers, Portugal's second tallest lighthouse and the Piscina das Mares, natural rock pools that are ideal for swimming when the Atlantic gets too rough.

Foz Velha

Formerly the fishermen's quarter, the most historic part of Foz do Douro is called **Foz Velha** (old Foz), and sits southeast of the seafront facing the Douro estuary; tram #1 runs here from the city centre, stopping along the riverfront at its southern edges. Today, Foz is distinctly upmarket, even sheltering a Michelin-starred restaurant, *Pedro Lemos* (see page 98), and its backstreets make for a great stroll past the pretty early eighteenth-century Igreja de Sao João de Douro and the affluent villas with their iron balconies.

Jardim do Passeio Alegre

MAP PAGE 92, POCKET MAP B13

Some of the nicest houses in Foz face onto the riverfront **Jardim do Passeio Alegre**, a pretty wedge-shaped park, which was laid out in the early twentieth century. Fringed by towering palms where troops of parakeets swoop and chatter, it has a couple of mini lakes, a children's play area, a mini golf course and a lively Sunday market, with stalls selling local produce and artisan products (10am–6pm).

The park is also home to most ornate toilets in Portugal, set in a beautifully tiled Art Nouveau pavilion; built in 1910, they are still in use today – check out the Ladies, with their Art Deco peacock tiles and an original restored toilet and sink dating from 1888 and painted in blue (you can't use this one, though, as it's just for show).

Getting to Foz

The most fun route to Foz is to take **tram #1** from Ribeira, which trundles up the riverfront to Foz Velha, a ten-minute walk from the sea. Alternatively, you can take **bus** #500 from São Bento; bus #502 from Bolhão to Parque de Cidade; bus #203 from Rotunda da Boavista via Serralves museum, to central Foz and Castelo do Queijo; or #200 from Bolhão to Castelo do Queijo.

Igreja de São João Baptista

MAP PAGE 92, POCKET MAP C13
Largo da Igreja ☎ 226 180 015. Free.
The small white seventeenth-century **church of São João Baptista** is known for its ornate altarpieces and impressive Baroque side altars, beautifully decorated with intricately designed gilt-wood carvings.

Farol de São Miguel-o-Anjo

MAP PAGE 92, POCKET MAP C13
Just southeast of the Jardim do Passeio Alegre, on a small promontory jutting into the river estuary, it is easy to overlook the squat, coarse-stone **Farol de São Miguel-o-Anjo**. However, this lighthouse is one of the oldest in Europe, dating back to 1528, when fires were lit at its summit to alert any approaching ships.

Castelo de São João Baptista

MAP PAGE 92, POCKET MAP B13
Esplanada do Castelo ☎ 226 153 440.
Just beyond the Jardim do Passeio Alegre, the confluence of river and ocean is dominated by the **Castelo de São João**, a sixteenth-century sea fort, which was one of the first to be built in a star shape. The sea fort was modified in the following century, but lost its strategic importance as the river shifted (it was originally situated right on the shoreline). Today, the Castelo de São João belongs to the National Defence Institute and is only open for occasional exhibitions: check with the tourist office (see page 127) for details of what's on. You can take a stroll around the mouth of the estuary here, along the sea walls that run behind the fort, a favourite spot for the local fishermen.

Foz seafront

Though it can't claim to have Portugal's best beaches, Foz's **seafront** still attracts plenty of visitors; take care, however, as the sand is interspersed with rocks, and the Atlantic is cold and can get pretty wild. At the seafront's southern end, you can walk up to the **Farol de Felgueiras** lighthouse.

Heading north, Avenida do Brasil and Avenida do Montevideu are packed with bars, restaurants and cafes. A boardwalk and promenade stretch all the way to

The wind-whipped Foz seafront

Forte de São Francisco Xavier

the Castelo do Queijo, just over 2km to the north, passing a series of coves: Praia do Molhe is the nicest. Along the promenade, you can stroll beneath the **Pergola da Foz**, built in the 1930s for the Mayor of Porto's wife, who had been so enchanted by the pergola on the Promenade des Anglais in Nice that she insisted that Porto should have its own. Here, too, is the **Homem do Leme statue**, dedicated to sea captains who navigate these tricky waters.

Mercado da Foz

MAP PAGE 92, POCKET MAP B12
Rua de Diu. Tues–Sat 7am–11pm, Mon 7am–5pm.

With its interesting local food stalls, the revamped **Mercado da Foz** is a good place to head for an inexpensive lunch. Like many others in Portugal, this small local market was struggling to survive, so has diversified: as well as the

Foz do Douro, Matosinhos & Leça da Palmeira

Pergola da Foz
Nevogilde, Matosinhos & Leça da Palmeira
FOR CONTINUATION NORTH SEE INSET MAP, BOTTOM LEFT

SHOPS		BARS AND CLUBS	
La Place Concept	2	Bar da Praia Homem do Leme	2
Padaria Formosa	1	Bar Tolo	1

Jardins da Avenida de Montevideu

FOR CONTINUATION NORTH SEE INSET MAP, FAR RIGHT

CAFÉS	
Brigadão	4
Casa Aberta	9
Casa de Pasto da Palmeira	11
Tavi	6

Leça da Palmeira (1.5km), Piscina das Mares (1.5km) & 13 (2.8km)

MERCADO (M)

Rio Leça

0 metres 250
0 yards 250

Homem de Leme

Mercado de Matosinhos

MATOSINHOS

RUA DO MOLHE
AVENIDA DO BRASIL

0 metres 250
0 yards 250

Pergola da Foz

FOR CONTINUATION SOUTH SEE MAIN MAP

Mercado do Peixe

0 metres 200
0 yards 200

RESTAURANTS	
A Capoeira	10
Bar Amarelo	12
Cafeína	3
Casa de Chá da Boa Nova	13
Casa Vasco	2
Dom Peixe	14
O Valentim	15
Pedro Lemos	7
Praia da Luz	5
Salto ó Muro	16
Tentações no Prato	8
Terra	1

usual vegetable, fish, meat and flower stalls, it has several small independent cafés and restaurants specializing in local produce and different dishes, from salads, wraps and just-squeezed juices, to sweets, a hamburger bar and the Famous Dog hot dog stall.

Castelo do Queijo

MAP PAGE 92
Praça do Gonçalves Zarco
☎ 226 181 067. Charge.

At the northern end of Foz's seafront is the large roundabout of Praça do Gonçalves Zarco, where you'll find the austere **Castelo de Queijo** (Cheese castle). Officially called the Forte de São Francisco Xavier, it was given its nickname because the rock it was built on resembles a giant cheese. The fort was built in 1661 to protect Porto's coastline from North African pirates, though was pressed into action in the 1830s when it was besieged by Dom Pedro's troops during the Portuguese civil war. Today, it houses a tiny military museum dedicated to Portugal's veterans who saw action in the former colonies of Angola and Mozambique, plus an exhibition space for displays of ceramics and paintings. It's all very low-key, however – the real draw is the sea views from the battlements above.

Sea Life Porto

MAP PAGE 92
1ª Rua Particular do Castelo do Queijo
🌐 visitsealife.com/porto. Charge.

Part of the Sea Life franchise, this **aquarium** makes a fun excursion, with sharks, rays, jellyfish, starfish and thousands of other creatures. Many of the tanks reflect the different ecosystems; there's one on the Douro River, which is home to freshwater species, plus a tropical bay of rays and an exhibit

FOZ DO DOURO, MATOSINHOS AND LEÇA DA PALMEIRA

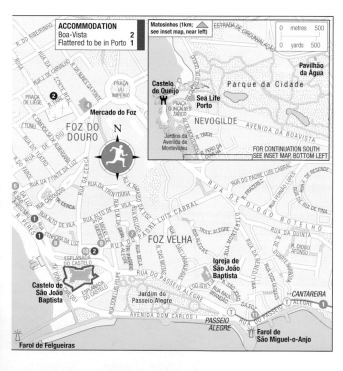

of giant spider crabs and lobsters. There are exotic species from Portugal's Atlantic islands, the Azores, plus an underwater tunnel through a tank where sharks and Mariza the turtle live. There are regular feeding times accompanied by informative talks.

Parque da Cidade

MAP PAGE 92
Entrance on Av da Boavista
☎ 225 320 080. Free.

Spreading inland from the seafront, the expansive **Parque da Cidade** is the largest urban park in Portugal, at just under a square kilometre. The park was opened in 2002, and today is peppered with paths that wend their way through lawned and wooded areas past four small lakes. Unsurprisingly, it's a popular spot for weekend picnics – come on a weekday and it feels far removed from the bustle of the city. There's also a garden centre here (located in the southwest corner), as well as farm buildings (in the northeast corner) with a Centre for Environmental Education and weekend activities for children.

Pavilhão da Água

MAP PAGE 92
Estrada da Circunvalação 15433
Ⓦ pavilhaodaagua.pt.

The shoe-box-like **Pavilhão da Água** (water pavilion) in the northeast section of the Parque da Cidade was built for the Lisbon Expo of 1998, but was moved here in the early 2000s. The Pavilhão da Água usually hosts imaginative displays and exhibits geared around the phases of the water cycle and their impact on the environment.

Matosinhos

Rua Heróis de França

Matosinhos' main claim to fame is as home to some of the region's finest fish and seafood restaurants, which cluster along Rua Heróis

Piscina das Mares, the highlight of Leça da Palmeira

Architecture and the Porto School

Long known for its innovative building design, Porto saw the emergence of its own style of contemporary architecture, with the so-called **Porto School** in the 1950s, centred on the city's School of Fine Arts. The Porto School proved fertile ground for many of the city's contemporary architects, including **Alcino Soutinho** (1930–2013), who worked on the conversion of the Casa-Museu Guerra Junqueiro (see page 37), and Amarante's Museu Amadeo de Souza-Cardoso (see page 108) and – most famously – local boy **Álvaro Siza Vieira** (born in 1933), whose masterpiece in Porto is the contemporary art museum at the Fundação Serralves. Earlier works by Siza Vieira can be seen in Leça da Palmeira, at the sublime sea pools and at the *Casa de Chá da Boa Nova* restaurant (see page 97). Siza Vieira won the Pritzker Prize (architecture's equivalent of the Oscars) in 1992, and his equally influential protégé, **Eduardo Souto Moura** (born 1952), followed suit and won it in 2011. Perhaps best known for his work on the remarkable football stadium at Braga, Souto Moura has also worked in his hometown of Porto at the Casa das Artes, and on the renovation of the city's Museu dos Transportes e Comunicações (see page 72).

Foz de Douro has become something of a hotspot for architecture, with both Souto Moura and his mentor Siza Vieira living in the town – indeed, architecture buffs can admire Souto Moura's skills close up, by staying in a house he designed in 2005, which is tucked away down Rua Padre Luís Cabral: it's available to let through ⓦ themodernhouse.com.

de França in the old quarter facing the fish market. Despite the earthy appearance of the street, people come for miles to dine here on top-quality fresh fish at reasonable prices.

Mercado dos Matosinhos

MAP PAGE 92
Rua França Júnior ⓣ 229 376 577. Mon 7am–2pm, Tues–Fri 6.30am–6pm, Sat 6.30am–4.30pm. Free. Ⓜ Mercado.
Matosinhos's **market** is one of the region's largest, set on two levels in a huge modern building with an impressive arched roof. Unsurprisingly, fish is the big thing here, with an astonishing array of sea creatures on sale, both familiar and bizarre. On the upper floor, you can find everything from fruit and vegetables, cakes and pastries, to caged rabbits and chickens.

Leça da Palmeira

Piscina das Mares

MAP PAGE 92
Av da Liberade, Leça da Palmeira
ⓦ matosinhosport.com. Charge.
The highlight of Leça da Palmeira lies at the northern end of its beach: the enticing **Piscina das Mares** (sea pools – with a separate one for kids), neatly carved out of the rocks beside the ocean. Opened in 1966, they were designed by local architect Álvaro Siza Vieira (see box, above), who was also responsible for the sleek *Casa de Chá da Boa Nova* (see page 97) another 2km up the seafront, one of the area's top restaurants. After renovations, the pools have now reopened, though note that they are seasonal (June–Sept).

Shops

La Place Concept

MAP PAGE 92, POCKET MAP B12

Rua do Faial 40, Foz do Douro

ⓦ pmfashionloft.com.

A large, stylish store with a luxury entrance showcasing local brands. Here you will find women's and children's clothing as well as shoes and decorative homeware.

Padaria Formosa

MAP PAGE 92, POCKET MAP A12

Rua de Gondarém 362, Foz do Douro

ⓦ padariaformosa.com.

This attractive, tiled-floor building houses one of Porto's oldest bakeries, dating from 1898. Sells home-made bread baked in a wood oven, plus cakes, pastries and pies.

Cafés

Brigadão

MAP PAGE 92, POCKET MAP B12

Mercado do Foz, Rua de Diu, Foz do Douro

ⓦ brigadao.pt.

Tiny café/shop selling an abundance of home-made traditional *brigadeiros* – small, truffle-like sweets made from condensed milk in a variety of flavours, including passion fruit, port, dark chocolate and churros. If one is not enough, you can buy a box to take away. €

Casa Aberta

MAP PAGE 92, POCKET MAP B13

Rua Padre Luís Cabral 1080, Foz do Douro

ⓣ 915 963 272.

With a bike hanging from the ceiling and a Vespa as part of the decor, this is typical of Foz's hip spaces: it's part boutique shop – selling toys, clothes and crafts – and part café, serving up moderately priced salads, sandwiches, scones and toasties. There's a small terrace at the back. €

Casa de Pasto da Palmeira

MAP PAGE 92, POCKET MAP C13

Rua do Passeio Alegre 450, Foz do Douro

ⓣ 911 074 336.

Fashionable café-restaurant with outdoor tables facing the Douro estuary. It's cosy inside and provides a range of teas, sharing plates, burgers and tapas. You can expect the likes of pork cheeks, *alheira*

Casa de Chá da Boa Nova perches on the rocky coastline

Beautiful sea views at *Tavi*

sausage or roasted octopus, though the menu changes monthly. €€

Tavi

MAP PAGE 92, POCKET MAP A12
Rua da Senhora da Luz 363, Foz do Douro
🕾 tavi.pt.
Foz's best café is always busy thanks to its wonderful sea-facing terrace and counter of amazing cakes. €

Restaurants

A Capoeira

MAP PAGE 92, POCKET MAP B13
Esplanada do Castelo 63, Foz do Douro
🕾 226 181 589.
In an attractive tiled building, this place serves reliable, traditional Portuguese dishes: fresh hake and sole cost; grilled turkey, veal or liver; and a variety of steaks. It's popular with locals, so get there early to bag a table. €€€

Bar Amarelo

MAP PAGE 92
Av Montevideu, Homen de Leme, Foz do Douro 🕾 226 182 963.
Unassuming local fish restaurant right on the beach, serving

traditional dishes in a simple dining room overlooking the sea, or on the large outdoor terrace. Expect the likes of fresh grilled sardines with tomato rice and grilled sea bass – regulars on the menu. €€

Cafeína

MAP PAGE 92, POCKET MAP A12
Rua do Padrão 100, Foz do Douro
🕾 cafeina.pt.
A beautiful traditional dining room with wooden floors, bookshelves on the walls and a homely vibe. It serves Portuguese dishes with an international twist such as cod gratin with onions, or stuffed squid. There's a good-value three-course lunch. €€€

Casa de Chá da Boa Nova

MAP PAGE 92
Av da Liberdade, Leça da Palmeira
🕾 casadechadaboanova.pt.
This stunning building, which seems to merge into the sea-facing rocks, was designed by Pritzer architect Ávaro Siza Vieria (see page 95) and is run by Michelin-starred chef Rui Paula (see page 78). As you'd expect, fish and seafood are the specialities,

with a few à la carte dishes and a choice of tasting menus: Earth and Sea bring together meat and fish, while Atlantic features the bounty of the ocean. All feature beautifully presented, innovative dishes that look as good as they taste. €€€€

Casa Vasco

MAP PAGE 92, POCKET MAP A12
Rua do Padrão 152, Foz do Douro
Ⓦ casavasco.pt.

A Scandi-style dining room, with grey wood walls and a pretty covered terrace, the "Basque House" is a cosy, informal restaurant serving good food. There's a tapas-style menu during the afternoon (3.30–7.30pm), with more substantial dishes served at lunchtime and in the evening, such as fish cooked on the grill, sea bass or seafood kebabs. €€€

Dom Peixe

MAP PAGE 92
Rua Heróis de França, Matosinhos 241
Ⓦ dompeixe.com.

One of the most highly rated of Matosinhos's seafood restaurants,

right opposite the fish market, this restaurant has a small outdoor terrace, slick service and a contemporary interior. Most fish is priced by the kilo: expect to pay around €12 for salmon, sardines or squid, around €15 for other fish. €€€

O Valentim

MAP PAGE 92
Rua Heróis de França, Matosinhos 263
Ⓦ ovalentim.com.

Run by the same team behind *Dom Peixe*, this is another fine Matosinhos fish restaurant. Catch of the day is cooked on an outside grill; expect the likes of John Dory, *espetada de tamboril* (monkfish kebab) and *açorda de camarão* (prawns cooked in a garlicky bread sauce). €€€

Pedro Lemos

MAP PAGE 92, POCKET MAP B13
Rua do Padre Luís Cabral 974, Foz do Douro
Ⓦ pedrolemos.net.

Tucked into an attractive backstreet of old Foz, this is a surprisingly small and cosy home

Terra occupies an attractive tiled building

for a Michelin-starred restaurant run by one of the city's most illustrious chefs. You'll have to book in advance for its five- or seven-course tasting menu, which features changing dishes depending on what's in season: some of the herbs and vegetables come from the outdoor terrace garden, which also has alluring shaded tables. Chef Pedro Lemos offers an original twist on largely local ingredients, and the menu may well feature the likes of chilled watermelon soup, tuna with asparagus, quail with mushrooms and sea bass with turnip and chestnuts. Everything is fresh and delicious, service is slick, and each dish can be paired with a fine wine, though expect to pay through the nose for the privilege. €€€€

Praia da Luz

MAP PAGE 92, POCKET MAP A12
Av do Brasil, Foz do Douro. ☎ 226 173 234.
Right on the sand and rock beach of the same name, this is a fab Foz chill-out spot, with lots of comfy chairs on terraces facing the waves. Considering its prime position, prices are reasonable, or you can easily ensconce yourself here with a drink to watch the sun set. €€€

Salto ó Muro

MAP PAGE 92
Rua Heróis de França 386, Matosinhos
☎ 229 380 870.
The "Jump the Wall" is an engaging, if cramped, family-run *tasca* on the dockside Matosinhos street, which is full of fish restaurants. Other places might look more enticing, but stick with it – a handwritten menu offers the catch of the day, plus some home-style specials (such as *arroz de polvo* or baked sardines). €€

Tentações no Prato

MAP PAGE 92, POCKET MAP B13
Rua Senhora da Luz 97, Foz do Douro
☎ facebook.com/TentacoesNoPrato.
This attractive tiled restaurant is run by a team of dedicated women who rustle up a small but tasty array of traditional Portuguese dishes such as grilled hake or octopus rice and *bacalhau*. The steak with beer sauce is recommended. It's very popular, so reserve in advance to avoid disappointment. €€

Terra

MAP PAGE 92, POCKET MAP A12
Rua do Padrão 103, Foz do Douro
☎ restauranteterra.com.
Hip and very popular restaurant occupying an attractive tiled building covered in eye-catching geometric designs. Inside, there are lots of exposed wood beams and tables on two floors of a surprisingly spacious restaurant, and the menu also springs a few surprises: along with the usual Portuguese grilled meat and fish, you'll find pasta dishes, risotto and even sushi, all made to a high standard. €€

Bars and clubs

Bar da Praia Homem do Leme

MAP PAGE 92
Av Montevideu 88, Foz do Douro
☎ 226 181 847.
Modern bar-café situated pretty much right on the beach, with fantastic sea views through huge glass windows and from the dining terrace in front. It serves cool drinks, light snacks, fresh salads and filling sandwiches.

Bar Tolo

MAP PAGE 92, POCKET MAP A13
Rua Senhora da Luz 185, Foz do Douro
☎ 224 938 987.
This tall, friendly café-bar spread across three floors serves tapas and a handful of daily specials. It can be a bit smoky on the ground floor so head up to the pretty roof terrace with serene views over the sea, or sit outside on the ground-floor patio.

Vila do Conde

To sample northern Portugal's beaches at their best, it is worth taking the swift metro ride up the coast to Vila do Conde. Set slightly inland on the river Ave, it's a historic town which grew up as an important shipbuilding centre, peered over by the majestic Convento de Santa Clara. Along with a shipbuilding museum, there's also an engaging embroidery museum boasting the world's largest piece of lace. Despite the old town attractions, however, it is the nearby beach, a fine swathe of soft golden sands, which pulls in most visitors.

The old town

Vila do Conde's old town clusters round the north bank of the Rio Ave, its riverfront lined with appealing cafés and restaurants. Anchoring the old town's cobbled alleys is the beautiful Manueline **Igreja Matriz**, with its impressive carved and gilded altar and tiled chapel. Begun in the late fifteenth century, the church was designed by João de Castilho, who was responsible for Seville's cathedral. In 1845, Portugal's greatest realist author, Eça de Queiroz was baptized in the church. Nearby, the Friday **market** (9am–6pm) takes place, where you'll find everything from farm produce to traditional children's toys.

Convento de Santa Clara

MAP PAGE 102
Largo Dom Afonso Sanches.
No public access.

The grand seventeenth-century **Convento de Santa Clara** is Vila do Conde's major landmark. Built to replace an earlier fourteenth-century monastery, the convent sits high above the old bridge and, while it's not open to the public, it is worth climbing up to the *miradouro* for sweeping views of the town and river. Running directly into the north side of the convent is a well-preserved, early eighteenth-century **aqueduct** which once carried water over a reputed 999 arches from Terroso, 5km north of town – the metro line to Póvoa do Varzim now cuts right through part of the remaining course. The other thing worth noting about the convent is its long tradition of pastry-making – the so-called *doces conventuais*, or convent cakes (see page 103), sickly sweet affairs that generally involve industrial quantities of sugar and eggs, and are now available in cafés and *patisseries* all over the town.

Getting to Vila do Conde

The easiest way to travel to Vila do Conde from Porto city centre is to take **metro** Line B. The stopping trains (1hr) call at Santa Clara, 300m east of the old town, and Vila do Conde, the same distance north of the old town. These services alternate with faster Express trains (50min, marked Exp), which only call at Vila do Conde. There are around four trains an hour (Mon–Fri), two–three an hour at weekends. You need a Zone 6 Andante card to travel this far.

Vila do Conde festivals

A good time to visit Vila do Conde is for the nine-day food fair **Feira de Gastronomia** (ⓦfeiradegastronomia.com), which takes place during the third week of August. There are around sixty stands set up in Jardim da Avenida Júlio Graça selling produce from around the country, from cakes and traditional pastries to olives, cheeses, pies and local liqueurs.

The same location also hosts the oldest craft fair in the country, the renowned **Feira Nacional de Artesanato** (ⓦfeiranacionaldeartesanato.com). From the last week of July to the first week of August, you can see local craftspeople selling their artisanal produce, including everything from baskets to lace and Portuguese guitars.

People also come from far and wide for **Curtas** (ⓦcurtas.pt), the European short-film festival held here for a week every July.

Museu de Rendas de Bilros

MAP PAGE 102
Rua de São Bento 70 ⓦviladoconde.com/
museu-das-rendas-de-bilros. Charge.

The town of Vila do Conde is also known for its traditional lacework and embroidery (*rendas de bilros*), and there is an active lacework school in the interesting **Museu de Rendas de Bilros**, a small museum housed in one of the town's old manor houses.

Rendilheiras (lacemakers) show off their skills here most days, surrounded by lovely examples of lacework and historic lace-making tools and equipment. Pride of place goes to what is officially the largest piece of lace in the world, which was made here by 150 lace-makers in 2015.

The piece consists of 440 squares of lace, each of which measure 30cm x 30cm. The museum is also a good place to buy hand-crafted lace, and you'll see more for sale in the local market and in shops around the town.

Convento de Santa Clara

Museu da Construção Naval

MAP PAGE 102

Largo da Alfândega ☎ 252 617 506. Charge, includes entry to Nau Quinhentista.

Vila do Conde's shipbuilding industry is among the oldest in Europe, and fishing boats reminiscent of fifteenth-century caravels are still constructed here, in the shipyards on the other side of the river. You can trace this heritage in the excellent **Museu da Construção Naval**, which is housed in the impressive former royal customs house, the Alfândega Régia (1487), located down by the riverfront. Inside, you can see waxwork figures of the former customs' men and smugglers and find information about the old customs house; there's also an exhibition on the history of ships since the seventeenth century with models and photos.

Nau Quinhentista

MAP PAGE 102

Largo da Alfândega ☎ 252 248 400. Charge, includes entry to Museu da Construção Naval.

Right on the riverfront is a replica of a sixteenth-century sailing vessel, which you can visit to get an idea of what it was like to live and work on a boat which once transported cargo from India. During the months at sea, the cramped ship would have been stuffed with supplies to keep the crew going.

Casa do Barco

MAP PAGE 102

Rua do Cais da Alfândega
☎ 252 248 445. Free.

The contemporary glass pavilion located right on the riverfront doubles as a regional tourist information office and a shop, with a small exhibition detailing the history of fishing.

Convent sweets

Portugal's tradition of **sweets and cakes** dates to the fifteenth and sixteenth centuries, when traders started to import sugar from plantations in the Portuguese colonies. It was an expensive commodity, and the Church was one of the few institutions that could afford to buy it. As a result, convents began to develop recipes for what became known as *doces conventuais*, or convent sweets, which they sold to make extra funds for Church coffers. The recipes often used sugar and egg yolks (the egg whites were used to starch the nuns' habits) and the resulting cakes were given slightly risqué names such as *Colchão de Noiva* (Bride's Mattress) and *Papos de Anjo* (Angel's Throats). The sweets are still made today using the traditional recipes, so if you want to sink your teeth into a *Barriga de Freira* (Nun's Belly), you can probably find one at the nearest *pastelaria*.

Capela do Socorro

MAP PAGE 102

Rua do Socorro. No set opening hours.

You can't miss the distinctive white Moorish dome of the sixteenth-century **Capela do Socorro** overlooking the riverside. Built in 1559 by Gaspar Manuel, a sailor and member of the Order of Christ, this unusual little chapel is completely round and deceptively plain from the outside. Its interior, however, is lined with impressive blue *azulejos* that depict scenes from the life of Christ, interrupted only by a vast wooden altar.

The beach

MAP PAGE 102

The **beach** is a fifteen-minute walk west of town, and boasts long stretches of wave-battered sands – be aware, though, that the Atlantic can be cold and rough even in August. To the south, the sands end at the mouth of the Rio Ave, marked by the seventeenth-century **Forte de São João Baptista**.

Bolo de mel, a local Portuguese cake

Café

O Forninho

MAP PAGE 102
Av Dr Artur Cunha Araujo 123
☎ 252 644 385.
This attractive café and bakery
is located right by the market
building and serves a good range of
cakes and pastries from a couple of
euros, as well as fresh bread. There
are also tables outside on the pretty
square. €

Restaurants

Adega da Vila

MAP PAGE 102
Rua Comendador António Fernandes da
Costa 57 ☎ 961 258 237.
Traditional brick-lined restaurant
with bottles and hams hanging
from the walls, wooden tables and
a few stools at the bar. It serves
authentic local tapas dishes, such
as octopus with green sauce or a
plate of clams, and you can choose
tasty accompaniments such as
wild rice. It's tiny, so you'll need to
book in advance. €€

Adega Gavina

MAP PAGE 102
Cais das Lavandeiras 56 ☎ 917 834 517.
Freshly caught fish and seafood
are all cooked outside on the
barbecue at this friendly restaurant
with a cosy, traditional interior
and tables outside overlooking the
river. The menu varies depending
on what has been caught that day,
but you can expect the likes of a
large sea bass for two people or
grilled octopus and tiger prawns,
washed down with a jug of fruity
house wine. €€

Aloha Surf Bar

MAP PAGE 102
Av Manuel Barros ☎ 252 618 886.
A lovely location right on the
seafront with comfy chairs and
tables on an outdoor terrace,
where you can watch the waves
breaking on the beach below. It's
smart, with contemporary decor
inside, and charges surprisingly
reasonable prices given its prime
position. The menu features a
selection of tapas-style dishes and
good-value larger dishes, such as
frango na brasa or a mixed meat
grill. The attached Aloha Surf

Adega da Vila, a tiny, traditional restaurant

Local favourite *Doca*

and SUP school ( alohasurfsup.com) takes out paddleboarding and surf groups and provides lessons. €€

Churrasqueira do Ave

MAP PAGE 102

Rua Comendador António Fernandes da Coasta 95 ☎ 252 633 391.

Simple, but serving up good food, this modern grill house has a scattering of tables outside, which fills with locals who come here for the barbecued dishes such as *frango*, a huge mixed meat grill or half a barbecued rabbit. If you fancy something lighter, then it also serves plates of black pork ham and local cheese. €€€

Doca

MAP PAGE 102

Rua Dr Elias de Aguiar 35/Largo do Ribeirinho 5 ☎ 936 025 994.

With a smart interior, this restaurant is very popular with the townsfolk for its tasty local dishes, such as *arroz de tamboril* (monkfish rice) and roast goat. The hearty lunch dish-of-the-day is excellent value and includes soup and a main – *bacalau com natas* (cod cooked in cream) perhaps – plus dessert or coffee. €€

Le Villageois

MAP PAGE 102

Praça da República 94 ⓦ grupobodegao.com.

With its attractive tiled interior and tables and chairs outside on the riverfront, this well-regarded restaurant specializes in fish dishes, such as grilled sea bass, squid and prawn kebabs, or *filletes de pescada*. €€€€

Republika

MAP PAGE 102

Praça da República ☎ 252 696 373.

Upmarket restaurant and tapas bar facing the river, with a varied menu featuring well-prepared meat and fish: steaks, grilled octopus and sumptuous tiger prawns. €€€€

Bar

Barcearia

MAP PAGE 102

1 Piso, Rua da Igreja 8
☎ 252 170 114.

Lively, popular bar/*cervejaria* with a nice outdoor garden and covered terrace. It serves a variety of fresh juices, milkshakes and simple food such as sandwiches, salad and mushroom *tostas*, and stays open till late.

Amarante

The small town of Amarante provides a taste of the best of rural northern Portugal, and makes for an appealing break from the bustle of Porto. The town is a delightful medley of tall handsome houses set either side of the Rio Tâmega, crossed by a picturesque arched stone bridge, the Ponte de São Gonçalo. Amarante's attractions include a bustling Wednesday and Saturday market, two impressive churches and a museum dedicated to the town's most famous artist, Amadeo de Souza-Cardoso. Throw in one of the country's top restaurants and the pleasant hour's journey from Porto through rolling verdant countryside, and it is well worth a day-trip.

The old town

Modern Amarante looks relatively sizeable on the approach; it has a population of around 56,000 and spreads up the slopes of the surrounding hills. Its quaint **old town, however,** nestles either side of the gently flowing Rio Tâmega (a tributary of the Douro), and can easily be explored in a morning or afternoon; although with one of the top hotels in the region and Michelin-starred restaurant *Largo do Paço* (see page 111), you may well be tempted to stay the night. The **market days** (Wednesday and Saturday 8am–1pm) are the liveliest, with fruit, veg and flower stalls filling the indoor market building, while traders selling cheap clothes, bags and traditional hats spill out onto the square outside. As the evening approaches, the local hooch, Gatão, a fruity *vinho verde*, can be enjoyed at one of the few late-opening esplanade bars found on the south side of the river near either of the town's bridges.

Ponte de São Gonçalo

The **Ponte de São Gonçalo**, the handsome arched bridge over the river Tâmega, dates back to the eighteenth century when it replaced an original structure that was said to have been built largely by hand

Getting to Amarante

The trip by bus (or car) from Porto to Amarante – which lies 60km away – takes less than an hour via the A4. Once you've cleared Porto's sprawling suburbs, the journey is an attractive one, taking you through bucolic rolling countryside and winding valleys that are lined with stepped terraces of vineyards. Regular Rodonorte services depart from Porto's Garagem Atlântico, which is located on Rua Alexandre Herculano near Praça da Batalha. The 9am Rodonorte service, returning at 3.30pm, makes for an ideal day-trip (see ⓦ rodonorte.pt for more details). In Amarante, the bus station is on Rua António Carneiro, which is a five-minute walk south of the river.

Gonçalo the hermit

The thirteenth-century saint, **São Gonçalo** was born into a wealthy family before deciding to become a priest and embark on a fourteen-year pilgrimage to the holy lands, during which time he left his nephew to guard his estate. Gonçalo's travels persuaded him to renounce worldly goods, and he looked so impoverished on his return that his nephew is said to have set dogs on him to chase him away. Gonçalo then decided to live as a hermit and build a bridge over the Tâmega, largely with his own hands. Soon, he began to perform miracles: when the labourers who were helping him with the construction ran out of wine, he is said to have hit a rock with a stick, after which wine flowed from under it. He is also said to have summoned fish out of the river for the workers to eat. Gonçalo subsequently became the town's patron saint, and after his death, Amarante became a destination for pilgrims. The saint's annual festival – known as the **Festas do Junho** – is celebrated over the first weekend in June, with the belief that Gonçalo's lasting miraculous powers can help find people a partner. This belief has also led to the traditional exchange of phallic cakes by unmarried couples.

by São Gonçalo (see page 107). The original bridge was destroyed after a flood in 1763.

The current bridge of Ponte de São Gonçalo played a prominent role in the Napoleonic Wars, when in 1809, Portuguese soldiers heroically used the river here to resist an invasion by French troops. At the time, the French had captured Porto, but were unable to cross the Tâmega at Amarante to link up with their troops in Spain because the Portuguese had mined the bridge. The Portuguese held out for fourteen days, until the French army took advantage of a foggy morning to disarm the fuse mechanism and storm the bridge. Taken by surprise, the Portuguese army fled in panic, but they had delayed the French long enough for Wellington's British troops to reach Lisbon, a move that eventually tipped the balance of power away from Napoleon's men.

Igreja de São Gonçalo

MAP PAGE 108
Praça da República. Free.

Cross the old stone Ponte de São Gonçalo over the Tâmega and you're confronted by the landmark **Igreja de São Gonçalo**, the most important church in Amarante. Construction started in 1540 under the reign of João III, on the spot where Gonçalo's hermitage once stood, although the holy site almost certainly dates

Ponte de São Gonçalo

back to pagan times. It took over fifty years and three more royals before construction of the church was complete: the facade features the Varanda dos Reis, displaying statues of the founding monarchs João III, Sebastião, Henrique and Felipe I. Inside the church, touching the saint's well-worn tomb allegedly brings forward the happy wedding day for hitherto thwarted lovers.

Museu Amadeo de Souza-Cardoso

MAP PAGE 108
Alameda Teixeira de Pascoaes
W amadeosouza-cardoso.pt.
Charge, under-15s free.

The remodelled Renaissance cloisters around the side of São Gonçalo church make an appealing backdrop for the **Museu Amadeo de Souza-Cardoso**, largely based around the Cubist and avant-garde works of Amadeo de Souza-Cardoso (1887–1918). Born and brought up in Amarante, he spent his formative years as an artist in Paris and Brussels, where he made friends with influential artists including Modigliani and Brancusi, and his works were exhibited in Germany and at the Armory Show in New York. He returned to Portugal but died young in the influenza pandemic of 1918.

He's still relatively little known outside Portugal, though a retrospective of his work was held in Paris in 2016. The absorbing collection in Amarante is well worth a look, his works using beautiful if muted colours. Look out for the intriguing *Water-mills* (1915) and the almost pixelated *Life of Instruments* (1915–16).

There are also amusing caricatures such as the *Caricature of Emmérico Nunes* (1910). The museum features works by

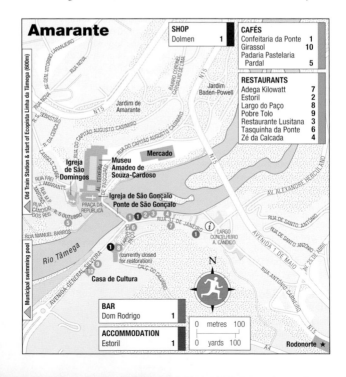

Igreja de São Gonçalo

other artists, too, including the Amarante-born Expressionist António Carneiro (1872–1930). There is also a programme of temporary exhibitions.

Igreja de São Domingos

MAP PAGE 108

Praça da República.

Free, charge for museum.

A steep granite stairway climbs from Amarante's main square, past the eighteenth-century **Igreja de** **São Domingos**, whose belltower chimes on the hour. Take a quick look inside the intimate chapel – by the door is an extraordinary carved wooden tablet showing Christ suspended upside down on the Cross, hoisted by three men operating a rope and pulley. The church also contains the small and mildly interesting Museu de Arte Sacra, with religious art from the sixteenth to the nineteenth century displayed across two floors.

Cycling along the Tâmega

In days gone by, the approach to Amarante was truly scenic, on the old Tâmega branch train line, with rattling wooden carriages snaking along a single-track route up the valley. Although long discontinued, part of the track now has a new lease of life as the **Ecopista da Linha do Tâmega**, a "green route" that's been opened from the old station at Amarante to that of Chapa, just over 9km to the northeast. In time, it's planned to extend the hiking and biking track as far as Celorico de Basto (22km from Amarante) and Arco de Baúlhe (40km), but even now, the shortish stretch to Chapa makes for a lovely day out, along the river valley, through pine and eucalyptus, over the occasional bridge and past abandoned buildings. You can hire bikes from the Casa Cultura at Avenida General Silveira 193 (ⓦ cm-amarante.pt).

Shop

Dolmen

MAP PAGE 108

Av General Silveira 59 Ⓦ dolmenco.pt.
Upmarket shop selling pricey but top-quality local handicrafts, including hand-embroidered serviettes and tablecloths, local cheese, olive oil, wine and honey.

Cafés

Confeitaria da Ponte

MAP PAGE 108

Rua 31 de Janeiro Ⓦ confeitariadaponte.pt.
The best place for coffee and cakes is right by the bridge, with a lovely riverside terrace. The nuns of the (now-ruined) Santa Clara convent once made the town's famous *doces*, and you can sample them here, including home-made *bolos de São Gonçalo* (saint's cakes) and *pão de ló* (sponge cake). €

Girassol

MAP PAGE 108

Casa Cultura, Av General Silveira 193
Ⓦ cm-amarante.pt.
Simple café in a youth centre with an attractive river terrace. It serves bargain vegetarian lunches then, after dark, it morphs into a bar and is popular with students. €

Padaria Pastelaria Pardal

MAP PAGE 108

Rua 5 Outubro 43 Ⓣ 255 423 019.
This pretty tiled *pastelaria* sells a great selection of cakes, breads and pastries to take away or eat in. The light and airy dining room with views over the river at the back also makes a good lunch spot – or you can sit at the tables on the street in front – for a bowl of soup and a sandwich, with freshly squeezed juices served in a jar. €

Restaurants

Adega Kilowatt

MAP PAGE 108

Rua 31 de Janeiro Ⓣ 255 433 159.
Tiny, traditional restaurant that's been in business for over eighty years, with tiled walls and smoked hams hanging from the bar. Squeeze inside for a tapas sharing plate of ham, sausage and cheese. €

Estoril

MAP PAGE 108

Rua 31 de Janeiro 150–152
Ⓣ 255 431 291.
This unassuming restaurant has a back terrace boasting lovely river views and is a tranquil spot for well-priced dishes such as local trout, sardines, grilled chicken and other grilled meats. €

Confeitaria da Ponte

Largo do Paço

Largo do Paço

MAP PAGE 108

Casa da Calcaola, Largo do Paço 6
Ⓦ largodopaco.com.

Michelin-star chef André Silva does
sublime things with local produce
in a series of tasting menus. Expect
a creative twist on tradition with
a seasonal edge, which in autumn
and winter might mean rabbit
stuffed with pistachios and served
with a mustard and herb crust or
roast pigeon with sautéed cherries.
€€€€

Pobre Tolo

MAP PAGE 108

Av General Silveira 169 Ⓦ pobretolo.pt.

Smart option on the riverfront
road opposite the old town, serving
regional cuisine: braised octopus,
monkfish rice and chicken in puff
pastry are all recommended, as are
the desserts. Mains are pricey, but
half-portions should suffice. There's
usually an inexpensive set lunch.
€€€€

Restaurante Lusitana

MAP PAGE 108

Rua 31 de Janeiro 65 ☎ 255 426 720.

Cosy place with tiled walls and a
balcony overlooking the river. It
serves good-value dishes such as
grilled salmon, plus specialities of
roast veal and *tripas à la moda da
casa* (tripe). €€

Tasquinha da Ponte

MAP PAGE 108

Rua 31 de Janeiro 193 ☎ 255 433 715.

Cosy downstairs place right by
the Ponte de São Gonçalo serving
simple good-quality home cooking
at bargain prices, and the menu may
feature the likes of grilled chicken
with chips and rice, bean and meat
stew or sardines with green beans. €

Zé da Calcada

MAP PAGE 108

Rua 31 de Janeiro 83 Ⓦ zedacalcada.com.

The nicest of the riverside choices
has a terrace with a river view and
serves good regional food, from
bacalhau to *posta á Maronesa* (hefty
steaks from the nearby Serra do
Marão). The good-value buffet
lunch offers a choice of hot and
cold dishes, including soup, coffee
and a drink. €€€

Bar

Dom Rodrigo

MAP PAGE 108

Rua 31 de Janeiro 39 ☎ 919 318 042.

The walls and tables of this tavern
are smothered with messages from
satisfied customers, and it's easy to
see why. Hams hang above the bar,
and you can choose from these,
smoked sausages or local cheeses,
washed down with a glass of wine. €

ACCOMMODATION

The outdoor pool at *The Yeatman*

Accommodation

Porto has been undergoing a tourism boom and has a wide range of accommodation to suit all budgets. Nevertheless, many places get booked up so it pays to reserve in advance. Nearly all the cheapest accommodation is in the city centre, while the boutique and smart accommodation tends to be in the medieval streets nearer the river. There are also good options in the upmarket suburbs of Boavista and out at the seaside in Foz do Douro: while the suburban location is a slight drawback, nowhere is much more than about thirty minutes' bus or metro ride from the centre. Only a few hotels have private parking, but some have cut-price deals with nearby car parks. There is also an increasing number of hostels (see page 118). Unless otherwise stated, all the prices quoted below are for the least expensive en-suite double room in high season, including breakfast. The Municipal Tourist Tax (€2 per night for all guests aged over 13) is not included in the prices stated here.

Ribeira

1872 RIVER HOUSE MAP PAGE 28, POCKET MAP D8. Rua do Infante Dom Henrique 133 Ⓦ 1872riverhouse.com. A beautifully renovated, eight-roomed townhouse on the riverfront – the building sits partly on the old city walls, which you can see through the breakfast room's glass floor. Contemporary rooms but with lots of original features, including stone walls and Art Deco tiles. The staff are super helpful, and the breakfasts excellent; served in a room with river views. You can help yourself to free coffee, tea and beer during the day. It's worth paying extra for a river-view room, though the streetview ones are just as quaint. €€€€

CARRIS PORTO MAP PAGE 28, POCKET MAP E7. Rua do Infante Dom Henrique 1 Ⓦ carris-porto-ribeira.hotel-rn.com. A few steps up the hill from the city's waterside, this stylish four-star hotel has been carved out of five old buildings, creating a dramatic lobby space made up of soaring stone arches and cutaway floors. Handsome rooms feature hardwood floors, earth-toned fabrics and bathrooms, while breakfast is served in a restaurant that sits beneath huge granite arches and pillars. €€€€

DESCOBERTAS BOUTIQUE HOTEL MAP PAGE 28, POCKET MAP E7. Rua Fonte Taurina 14 Ⓦ descobertasboutiquehotel.

Author picks

LUXURY *The Yeatman* see page 116
BOUTIQUE *Flores Village* see page 116
TRADITIONAL *Grande Hotel de Paris* see page 116
BUDGET *Duas Nações* see page 116
FAMILY-FRIENDLY *Flattered to be in Porto* see page 119

Accommodation price codes

Throughout the Guide, accommodation is categorized according to a price code, which roughly corresponds to the following price ranges. Price categories reflect the cost of a double room, without breakfast, in peak season.

€€€€	over €250
€€€	€180–250
€€	€120–180
€	under €120

com. This comfortable boutique-style hotel is situated in a narrow cobbled street, just one block back from the riverfront. In a renovated old building, the eighteen rooms are comfortable and stylish and the decor, in a nod to the Portuguese Discoveries, has some ethnic touches. €€

GUEST HOUSE DOURO MAP PAGE 28, POCKET MAP D8. Rua Fonte Taurina 99 Ⓦ guesthousedouro.com. This super-cool waterfront B&B has windows right on the Douro. Not all the rooms have river views (some look over the medieval street outside instead), but there's a sharp sense of style throughout and you couldn't get closer to the action. There's also parking nearby. Closed early January. €€€

INPATIO GUESTHOUSE MAP PAGE 28, POCKET MAP D7. Pátio de São Salvador 22, off Rua Mouzinho da Silveira 64 Ⓦ inpatio. pt. This renovated nineteenth-century house is tucked away in a tranquil patio: the comfortable, contemporary rooms are set over three floors, with kettles (something of a rarity in Portugal), bright white decor and grey slate bathrooms complete with Fair Trade toiletries. The superb breakfast features fresh local bread, pastries and cheeses as well as a different, though equally tasty, home-made cake served each day. €€

PESTANA VINTAGE PORTO MAP PAGE 28, POCKET MAP E8. Praça da Ribeira 1 Ⓦ pestana.com. Enjoying the Ribeira's best location, atop the medieval wall next to the river, this cluster of old buildings has been transformed into a boutique-style four-star hotel. Rooms are plush if not huge, and most face the Douro (corner rooms also overlook the Ponte de Dom Luís I bridge). €€€€

The Sé and Aliados

AMÉRICA MAP PAGE 38, POCKET MAP H1. Rua de Santa Catarina 1018 ☎ 22 339 2930. Ⓜ Faria Guimarães or Trindade. Located in a slightly run-down area towards the top of Rua de Santa Catarina, the *América* is a well-regarded mid-range choice with bright and relatively spacious rooms, though there can be some street noise. There is also private underground parking and a bar. €€

CASTELO DE SANTA CATARINA MAP PAGE 38. Rua de Santa Catarina 1347 Ⓦ castelosantacatarina.com. Ⓜ Faria Guimarães or Marquês or bus #701/#702/ #703 from Mercado do Bolhão. A 35min walk from the centre, this dramatic turreted folly was built at the end of the nineteenth century by a wealthy textiles merchant and now houses a modest guesthouse. The comfortable rooms aren't grand or expensive, but are furnished in period style, while breakfast is eaten in the lush *azulejo*-tiled gardens. There's parking, but no bar. €€

GRANDE HOTEL DO PORTO MAP PAGE 38, POCKET MAP G4. Rua de Santa Catarina 197 Ⓦ grandehotelporto.com. Ⓜ Bolhão. Porto's oldest hotel is steeped in nineteenth-century mercantile style, with polished marble and crystal chandeliers, and an echoing gilt-tinged restaurant where breakfast is served. It's in a handy location, on the main pedestrianized shopping street. Rooms are not huge but have contemporary decor, and prices are pretty good, especially during special promotions. There's limited parking and a small gym. €€

NH COLLECTION MAP PAGE 38, POCKET MAP G5. Praça da Batalha

60–65 W nh-hotels.com. M São Bento.
A swanky modern hotel in a renovated
eighteenth-century palace. It's perhaps a
little corporate but it benefits from a great
location. The rooms (and beds too) are
spacious with flatscreen TVs, and some
overlook the Praça de Batalha. There's also
a range of good facilities, including a gym,
spa and indoor pool. €€€

PESTANA PALÁCIO DO FREIXO MAP
PAGE 38. Estrada Nacional 108
W pestanacollection.com. **No metro or
buses run here: a taxi into the town centre
costs around €15.** A couple of kilometres
east of the city centre in a majestic
riverside location is the magnificently
restored Baroque *Palácio do Freixo*. Dating
back to 1742, the main period-style
building houses an elegant restaurant,
bar and public rooms, while contemporary
bedrooms – many with classic river views –
are set in an adjacent former flour factory.
There's an outdoor infinity pool with river
views, and you can also enjoy the indoor
pool and spa. €€€

The Baixa

DUAS NAÇÕES MAP PAGE 50, POCKET
MAP D4. Praça Guilherme Gomes
Fernandes 59 W hotelduasnacoes.com.
M Aliados. Don't be fooled by the run-down
exterior; this budget gem has updated
double-glazed rooms with satellite TV
and central heating. It's popular with
backpackers, as some bunk-style rooms
sleep four. Double rooms are also offered:
book ahead if you want a private bathroom.
No credit cards. €

GRANDE HOTEL PARIS BY STAY HOTELS
MAP PAGE 50, POCKET MAP E4. Rua
da Fábrica 27–29 W stayhotels.pt/
grandehotelparis. M Aliados. Opened
in 1877, the *Grande Hotel Paris* is more
a guesthouse and has been frequented
by Portugal's finest writers and artists,
including Eça de Queiroz and poet Guerra
Juncqueiro. Now under the Stay Hotels
umbrella, the building retains many
original fittings, with period furniture
and high ceilings, a small garden and
a good breakfast served in a splendid
drawing room. Rear rooms have balconies

and old-town views, and there are also
interconnecting rooms for families. €€€

INFANTE SAGRES MAP PAGE 50, POCKET
MAP E4. Praça Dona Filipa de Lencastre
62 W hotelinfantesagres.pt. M Aliados.
A glamorous, contemporary design hotel
with antique Persian carpets, crystal
chandeliers, Chinese porcelain and stained-
glass windows, which complement the
funky Portuguese custom-made furniture
and chic cosmopolitan style. There's an
open-air patio, bar and good restaurant and
relaxed spa, plus parking nearby. €€€

OCA FLORES HOTEL BOUTIQUE MAP PAGE
50, POCKET MAP E6. Rua das Flores 139
W ocahotels.com/hoteles/oca-flores-
hotel-boutique. M São Bento. On the
fashionable, pedestrianized Rua das Flores,
this boutique hotel is a clever conversion of
an eighteenth-century townhouse, with five
storeys at the front, and a hidden garden
off the fourth floor at the back. The rooms
are spacious and modern – those on the
top floor have the best views over the city.
There's even an atmospheric pool, secreted
in the villa's former wine cellars, and full
spa facilities, while a generous buffet
breakfast is served in a grand room off the
gardens. Good low-season deals. €€€€

PÃO DE AÇÚCAR MAP PAGE 50,
POCKET MAP E4. Rua do Almada 262
W paodeacucarhotel.pt. M Aliados. A fab
Art Deco survivor from the 1940s that was
once the favoured hotel of visiting artistes,
including fado diva Amália Rodrigues. While
the rooms could do with a style injection,
they have shiny parquet floors and a
fair amount of space. The best rooms on
the top floor open onto a private terrace
overlooking the town hall. The amazing
spiral staircase also contains a collection
of historic bumper cars, retrieved from a
former fairground. €€€

Vila Nova de Gaia

HOUSE OF SANDEMAN MAP PAGE
62. Largo Miguel Bombarda 67
W thehouseofsandeman.pt. M Jardim do
Morro. Wine-themed hostel with budget-
friendly dorms and a clutch of private
rooms. The walls are hung with artwork

from the Sandeman wine brand, whose cellars are a short hop away for tastings. **Dorms €, doubles €€**

THE YEATMAN MAP PAGE 62. **Rua do Choupelo** Ⓦ **the-yeatman-hotel.com.** Ⓜ **General Torres.** Porto's top hotel sits amid the historic port wine lodges, with fantastic views over the city and river from the gardens and all the rooms, many with spacious terraces. Both the infinity pools – one indoors with a luxurious spa, the other a decanter-shaped outdoor pool – have amazing panoramic views, too. The hotel is home to Portugal's top Michelin-starred restaurant (see page 70), and guests get a private tour with the sommelier of its wine cellar, housing one of the world's best collections of Portuguese wines. Visiting football teams playing FC Porto often stay here, and one of the corridors displays a series of signed players' shirts, including Maradona and Ronaldo. Rates vary considerably throughout the year. **€€€€**

Miragaia and Massarelos

EUROSTAR DAS ARTES MAP PAGE 74, POCKET MAP B3. **Rua do Rosário 160–164** Ⓦ **eurostarshotels.co.uk/eurostars-das-artes.html.** Ⓜ **Aliados.** The facade of a handsome tiled building in the heart of this fashionable district shelters a modern, contemporary hotel with rooms in two blocks – one for doubles and one for twin rooms. It's mostly geared towards business travellers, so is slightly anodyne, but the rooms are comfortable, and there's a bar and small patio garden. **€€**

PENSÃO FAVORITA MAP PAGE 74, POCKET MAP B3. **Rua de Miguel Bombarda 267** Ⓦ **pensaofavorita.pt.** Ⓜ **Aliados.** A winding, vertiginous staircase leads to a clutch of white, minimalist guest rooms, with high ceilings, gleaming wood floors and crisp white bedlinens. There's a sun-kissed garden and a popular basement restaurant, too. **€€**

PORTA AZUL MAP PAGE 74, POCKET MAP A4 & D10. **Rua Dom Manuel II 204** ☏ **224 037 706. Bus #200 from Av Aliados.** The "Blue Door" is a small, welcoming guesthouse right by the Jardim do Palácio de Cristal. Great value, it has just six guest rooms, most of which have a balcony overlooking, or with direct access to, a pretty, sheltered garden. **€**

ROSA ET AL TOWNHOUSE MAP PAGE 74, POCKET MAP B3. **Rua do Rosário 233** Ⓦ **rosaetal.pt.** Ⓜ **Aliados or Trindade.** Six boutique-style elegant suites occupy an impressively restored townhouse in an artsy, residential district near the Soares dos Reis museum. There's afternoon tea and regular classes, such as one on Portuguese gastronomy. All rooms come with hardwood floors, warm lighting and classy bathrooms with clawfoot bathtubs, and some rooms have balconies. **€€€**

VINCCI PORTO MAP PAGE 74, POCKET MAP A10. **Alameda de Basílio Teles 29** Ⓦ **vincciporto.com. Tram #1 from Ribeira.** Right on the riverfront, facing the Douro, this four-star hotel is in an imaginatively converted former fish market; breakfast is served in the high-ceilinged former main market area. Rooms are spacious and contemporary, and there's a bar, restaurant and free parking. **€€**

Boavista

CASA DO CONTO MAP PAGE 84. **Rua da Boavista 703** Ⓦ **casadoconto.com.** Ⓜ **Carolina Michaelis.** The *Casa do Conto* displays an impressive conversion of a nineteenth-century house into contemporary and architecturally interesting apartments, most with writing on the ceiling. Each apartment is slightly different, but all are bright and spacious with kitchenettes and contemporary facilities, and the top-floor room comes with its own balcony. **€€**

HOTEL DA MÚSICA MAP PAGE 84. **Mercado do Bom Sucesso, Largo Ferreira Lapa 21** Ⓦ **hoteldamusica.com.** Ⓜ **Casa da Música.** Located in the Bom Sucesso Market and conveniently close to the Casa da Música, this sleek design hotel has 85 rooms spread across its four floors. The en-suite rooms are all musically themed and inspired by local and international composers. There's also a chic bar as well as a decent hotel restaurant. **€€**

Foz do Douro

BOA-VISTA MAP PAGE 92, POCKET MAP B13. Esplanada do Castelo 58, Foz do Douro Ⓦ hotelboavista.com. Tram #1 from Ribeira or bus #500 from São Bento. Ocean and river views are the thing at this traditional villa, set over the road from the fort at Foz do Douro – it's worth paying extra (and booking in advance) for a waterview room. Rooms are comfortable if unexceptional, but there's a fine rooftop pool and sun terrace, plus bar, restaurant and parking. €€

Vila do Conde

QUINTA DAS ALFAIAS MAP PAGE 102. Rua da Trás 220, Fajozes, 10km southeast of town ☎ 252 662 146. A wonderfully elegant nineteenth-century country house set in extensive gardens and orchards, with a swimming pool and tennis court. It has four en-suite rooms with garden views, plus two suites and apartments sleeping four or six – the decor understated, with plenty of bare granite, and the style is traditional country house. €€

Amarante

ESTORIL MAP PAGE 108. Rua 31 de Janeiro 49 ☎ 255 431 291. A star pick for budget travellers – pleasant, high-ceilinged en-suite guest rooms and, for a few euros more, a balcony overlooking the river and bridge. Breakfast isn't included, but the cheery attached restaurant is a firm favourite for inexpensive riverside terrace dining. €

Hostels

Porto's hostels have improved dramatically over the last few years, and many are chic and comfortable, with facilities on a par with (or better than) some hotels. Prices start at €20 for dorms and around €45 for a double room – about half the cost of the least expensive hotel. A youth hostel card is required for the official youth hostel (pousada da juventude) – you can buy one on your first night's stay. Unless stated, prices don't include breakfast.

BLUESOCK HOSTEL MAP PAGE 28, POCKET MAP E7. Rua de São João 40 Ⓦ bluesockhostels.com. Ⓜ São Bento. Hostel in a blue-tiled building, with traditional stone walls, wooden beams and modern facilities. The well-designed dorms (both mixed and female-only) have spacious bunks with charger points, lockers and curtains: there are also en-suite doubles and twins, plus a rooftop suite with breathtaking views. The friendly staff organize pub crawls and fado nights, and there's a lively bar in the vaulted cellar. Breakfast is included. **Dorms €, doubles €€, suite €€€€**

PILOT DESIGN HOSTEL MAP PAGE 50, POCKET MAP D3. Largo Alberto Pimentel 11 Ⓦ pilothostel.com. Ⓜ Trindade. This friendly, funky hostel is in a good location close to one of the main nightlife areas, though it also has its own late-opening bar. It has various small but comfy dorms sleeping four to twelve guests, and there's a small back patio. It arranges various events including walking tours and pub crawls. **€**

PORTO ALIVE MAP PAGE 50, POCKET MAP E6. Rua das Flores 138 ☎ 220 937 693. Ⓜ São Bento. Well located in a fashionable, pedestrianized street, this hostel has eight- or ten-bed dorms, which are contemporary though a bit small. There are double rooms too (with shared bathroom, including one with a balcony, as well as a communal kitchen and living room. **Dorms €, doubles €€**

PORTO GALLERY HOSTEL MAP PAGE 74, POCKET MAP B3. Rua de Miguel Bombarda 222 Ⓦ gallery-hostel.com. Ⓜ Aliados or Trindade. In trendy Rua Miguel Bombarda, this renovated, family-run, 1906 townhouse has luxury en-suite four- and six-bed dorms plus double rooms. It hosts local artists' exhibitions, and the chill-out area has a small bar and living room with garden. **Dorms €, doubles €€**

POUSADA DE JUVENTUDE MAP PAGE 84. Rua Paulo da Gama 551, Pasteleira, 4km west of the centre ⓦ pousadasjuventude.pt. Bus #504 from Ⓜ Casa da Música, or #500 from São Bento. It's a bit of a way out and not ideal for night owls, but most of the doubles and dorms in Porto's contemporary hostel have wonderful views of the Douro. There's also a self-contained apartment sleeping four. Book ahead in summer. **Dorms €, doubles €€, apartments €€€**

RIVOLI CINEMA HOSTEL MAP PAGE 38, POCKET MAP F4. Rua Dr Magalhães Lemos 83 ⓦ rivolicinemahostel.com. Ⓜ Aliados or Trindade. Co-owned by a bunch of art-grad, movie-crazy friends, this bright, airy townhouse has film-themed dorms and double rooms, all sharing toilets and showers. It's funky and communal – one big breakfast table, a kitchen, lounge and outdoor roof terrace – and they organize events like poker nights and evening drinks. **€**

Self-catering

There are some good options for self-catering in Porto, which often works out cheaper than a hotel, especially for groups or families. Along with the places listed below, try ⓦ airbnb.co.uk or ⓦ flatinporto.com.

BAUMHAUS MAP PAGE 84. Rua da Boavista 781 ⓦ baumhaus.pt/baumhaus. Ⓜ Carolina Michaelis. A nineteenth-century townhouse that has been transformed into nine self-catering apartments on five floors (one in the loft), each named after a Portuguese artist. The rooms have modern Scandi-style decor with all amenities and appliances, and there's a lovely garden with a barbecue area for the summer evenings. **€€**

FLATTERED TO BE IN PORTO MAP PAGE 92, POCKET MAP A13. Rua Senhora da Luz 145 ⓦ flatteredapartments.com/porto. Light, airy, spacious apartments, some with fantastic sea views, in an old, beautifully renovated seaside house. The location is great – a stone's throw from both the beach and the cafés and restaurants of the old town. The apartments are modern, stylish and comfortable, with a well-equipped kitchenette; highly recommended. **€€€**

THE PORTO RIVER APARTHOTEL MAP PAGE 28, POCKET MAP E7. Rua dos Canastreiros 50 ⓦ portoriver.pt. In a great position, just back from the riverfront, this is a good option for self-caterers. The bright, white rooms (from studios to two-bed apartments) have small kitchenettes and bathrooms, though the price includes breakfast. It's worth paying extra for river views, as the back rooms overlook a narrow alley. **€€€**

OCA VITÓRIA VILLAGE MAP PAGE 50, POCKET MAP D5. Rua das Flores 139 ⓦ ocahotels.com/hoteles/oca-vitoria-village. Ⓜ São Bento. With a separate entrance on Rua da Vitoria and sharing all the facilities of the *Flores Village* (see page 116), the *Oca Vitória Village* offers spacious self-catering duplex apartments, some of which open directly onto the gardens. These are excellent for families, the largest sleeping up to six guests, with well-equipped kitchens. **€€€**

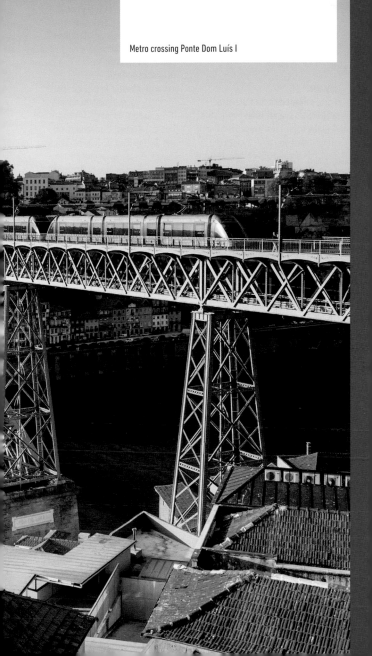

ESSENTIALS

Metro crossing Ponte Dom Luís I

Arrival

Porto's airport is located 13km north of the city and is well served by the metro and taxis. The city's train stations are connected to the metro while the various bus stations are all centrally located.

By air

Porto's **Francisco Sa Carneiro airport** (ⓦana.pt) is on Metro Line E (daily 6am–1am, every 20–30min), which takes you directly into the centre in around 30–45 minutes – to Casa da Música (for Boavista hotels), Trindade, Aliados or Bolhão (for city-centre hotels), or São Bento or Campanhã (for onward train services). Taxis from the airport into the centre cost €20–30; make sure you get one from the authorized rank outside the terminal.

By train

Portugal's **trains** are run by CP (Comboio de Portugal ⓦcp.pt). International, intercity and ALFA Pendular trains arrive at the **Estação de Campanhã**, 2km east of the city centre. With a ticket to Porto, you can simply change here onto any local train for the central São Bento station, a five-minute ride away. Campanhã is also on the metro, or it's a short taxi ride into the centre. The **Estação de São Bento** is the city-centre station for suburban and regional services, and for connections to intercity and international services from Campanhã. There's a metro station here and taxis outside. You can buy tickets for any train at São Bento (even for Campanhã departures).

By bus

Buses to Porto arrive at various stops and garages all over the city, though most are fairly central.

Eurolines (international services) use the **Internorte terminal** at Praça da Galiza (ⓦinternorte. pt, ⓜCasa da Música). **Garagem Atlântico**, Rua Alexandre Herculano, near Praça da Batalha, is a hub for several companies including the national operator Rede Expressos (ⓦrede-expressos.pt); Rodonorte (Estremadura, Ribatejo, Minho, Trás-os-Montes; ⓦrodonorte.pt) and Santos (Beiras, Trás-os-Montes, Lisbon; ⓦsantosviagensturismo .pt) stop on Rua Ateneu Comercial, near Bolhão market; while Renex (Estremadura, Ribatejo, Lisbon, Algarve and Minho; ⓦrenex.pt) stop at Campo dos Mártires da Pátria 37, next to the Palácio da Justiça.

By car

Driving into Porto is to be avoided if possible – the city centre is congested and the one-way system confusing. You don't need a car to see the city, so the best advice is to park where you can use public transport. Major suburban metro stations have **parking** – particularly at the football stadium, Estádio do Dragão – or use one of the sign-posted city-centre car parks or garages; following signs for "Centro" or "Aliados" will send you into the maelstrom. Garage parking is expensive, but you'll have little choice if your hotel doesn't have parking, as on-street metered parking is limited to two hours (though it's free after 8pm and over the weekend).

For **car rental**, most international companies have both downtown and airport offices; if you need a vehicle for exploring further afield it's far easier to pick up your car the day you leave Porto. Local companies include Guerin (ⓦguerin.pt).

Getting around

You'll be able to walk – more like climb – between all the city-centre attractions, but you'll have to use public transport to get out to the Fundação Serralves museum, the coast and the airport. There's an extensive bus network and a swift metro system, while a funicular and three vintage tram lines still remain in service. The local transport authority, STCP (Ⓦstcp.pt), has a useful website and offices in Campanhã train station and Casa da Música and Trindade metro stations. A **river taxi** (see page 127) connects Ribeira and Vila Nova de Gaia, docking near the Sandeman port wine lodge.

The metro

The modern **metro** system (Ⓦmetrodoporto.pt) currently runs on six lines, A to F, underground in the city centre and then overground to the airport and to suburban destinations. Two new routes are in the works: Line G (Pink Line) is expected to come into service in 2024/25 and will connect Casa da Música to São Bento through Cordoaria; Ruby Line H, set to enter service in 2026, will run between Casa da Música and Santo Ovídio in Vila Nova de Gaia (the project will include a new bridge over the Douro).

You need an Andante card (see page 124) to use the system. Other than for the ride in from the airport or for the trip up the coast to Matosinhos or Vila do Conde, the metro isn't particularly useful for sightseeing, though there are handy city-centre stops at Trindade, Aliados, Bolhão and São Bento.

You can also use it to go to the Casa da Música at the Rotunda da Boavista and FC Porto's stadium, Estádio do Dragão. A spectacular ride to experience is Line D (from Trindade, Aliados or São Bento), which crosses the river to Vila Nova de Gaia along the top tier of Ponte de Dom Luís I.

Buses and trams

Buses and **trams** are also run by STCP. Major city bus stops include Praça Almeida Garrett opposite São Bento station, Praça da Liberdade at the bottom of Avenida dos Aliados, Jardim da Cordoaria and the interchange at Casa da Música metro station.

Porto's trams (*eléctricos*) run 5km from Ribeira along the river to Foz do Douro (25min), with a branch from the Igreja do Carmo at Cordoaria in the city centre (using this, change halfway at Massarelos, by the tram museum). The

Useful bus routes

#500 from São Bento to the coast at Matosinhos via Ribeira, the Museu Vinho do Porto and Foz do Douro.
#502 from Bolhão to Matosinhos via Cedofeita, Boavista, Estádio de Bessa and Castelo do Queijo.
#207 from Campanha station to the Fundaçao de Serralves via the bus station, Aliados, Jardim do Palácio de Cristal and the Pousada de Juventude (youth hostel).
#208 from Aliados to Casa da Música and Boavista via Jardim do Palácio de Cristal.
#303 A circular route to and from Batalha via São Bento station, Torre dos Clérigos, Jardim da Cordoaria, Museu Nacional Soares dos Reis, Jardim do Palácio de Cristal, Casa da Música and Boavista.

Travel cards and tourist passes

To use the metro – and to save money on other forms of public transport – you need a rechargeable **Andante card**, which costs €0.60 and is available from ticket machines and from other marked Andante shops and kiosks (Lojas Andante). You credit the card with one, two or ten trips – the whole region is divided into concentric colour-coded zones, though everywhere you're going to want to go in Porto all falls within the same central zone 2. A single trip in the central zone costs €1.20 – you can change transport for free within the hour. It sounds complicated, but in practice it isn't, and you can change the instructions on the machines in every station to English.

If you're doing a lot of travelling, buy an **Andante Tour pass** (€7 for 24hr, €15 for 72hr), which is valid on all metros, buses and local trains. The pass is available on arrival at the airport from the Tourism Office in the Arrivals Hall.

If you are planning some intensive sight-seeing, the *turismos* also sell the **Porto Card** (€13 one day; €20 two days; €25 three days; €33 four days), which gives unlimited bus, metro and funicular travel plus discounts or free entry at many museums and monuments, wine cellars, bars, restaurants and shops. There are also streamlined versions (with no transport included) for €6, €10 or €13.

service operates daily (9.15am–7pm; departures every 30min). You can either buy a flat fare or get a 48hr ticket.

Funicular

The quickest way from the city centre down to Ponte de Dom Luís I (for Vila Nova de Gaia) and Ribeira is via the **Funicular** (or *elevador*) **dos Guindais** (every 10min: April–Oct Sun–Thurs 8am–10pm, Fri & Sat 8am–midnight; Nov–March Sun–Thurs 8am–8pm, Fri & Sat 8am–10pm).

Taxis

A typical taxi ride across town costs €10–15, and most squares and major stations have taxi ranks (or call Taxi Porto ☏ 225 997 336). Uber is also available in Porto.

By bike

Porto's extremely hilly and often cobbled terrain might make **cycling** seem like a no-no, but the Douro riverside actually makes a fine cycle way on both the north and south banks, with the most obvious routes being those that head out to the sea at Foz do Douro (or Afurada on the south side of the river). Bike hire is available from Biclas 7 Triclas near the north riverside at Rua da Arménia 30 (ⓦ tricla.pt; daily 9am–8pm).

Road train

A **road train** trundles from the Sé to Vila Nova da Gaia (May–Sept roughly every 30min 9.30am–6pm, Oct–April hourly 10am–5pm; ⓦ magictrain.pt; the fare includes a tasting at a port lodge).

Directory A–Z

Accessible travel

Buses, metros and trains have access for people with disabilities (though not the trams). Public buildings are obliged to have accessible entry for visitors, though be aware that many of Porto's streets are very steep and often cobbled. Disabled Holidays (ⓦdisabledholidays.com) can arrange specialist holidays staying at accessible hotels. The main Portuguese tourism office also has a comprehensive section on disabled travel at ⓦvisitportugal.com/en/experiencias/turismo-acessivel, including a list of accessible hotels, attractions and restaurants.

Addresses

Addresses are written in the form "Rua do Crucifixo 50–4°", meaning the fourth storey of no. 50, Rua do Crucifixo. The addition of e, d or r/c at the end means the entrance is on the left (*esquerda*), right (*direita*) or on the ground floor (*rés-do-chão*).

Children

Portugal is very child-friendly, and kids are welcomed pretty much anywhere. Supermarkets sell nappies and pharmacies sell baby food and formula milk. However, Porto's steep and often cobbled streets aren't ideal for pushchairs and the sun can be very strong.

Cinema

Mainstream films are shown at various multiplexes around the city, usually with Portuguese subtitles, and tickets are usually around €10. Listings can be found on ⓦfilmspot.pt. One of the most central options is the wonderful Art Deco Cinema Trindade on Rua do Almada 412 (ⓦcinematrindade.pt).

Crime

For English-speaking police assistance go to the Esquadra de Turismo (Tourism Police Department), a branch of the PSP, at Rua Clube dos Fenianos 11, next to the main *turismo* (☎222 081 833).

Violent crime is very rare, but pickpocketing is common, especially on public transport.

Electricity

Portugal uses two-pin plugs (220–240v). UK appliances will work with a continental adaptor.

Health

Pharmacies, the first point of call if you are ill, are usually open Monday to Friday 9am–1pm & 3–7pm, Saturday 9am–1pm. One of the most central options, Farmácia Parente on Rua das Flores 116, is also open on Saturday afternoon. Late-night and 24hr pharmacies (*farmácias de serviço*) operate on a rota basis; details are posted in the windows and given in the daily *Jornal de Notícias*, or call ☎118.

Hospital Santo António, Porto's main hospital, is located on Largo Prof Abel Salazar, near the university (☎222 077 500, ⓦchporto.pt).

Internet

Wi-fi is available, usually for free, in most cafés, restaurants, hotels and public spaces. You can also usually use computers in libraries, hotels and hostels, also usually without charge.

For most European mobile providers, you are able to use your own subscription without extra costs, otherwise there are companies like Portugal Internet (ⓦportugalinternet.com) which can help you out with internet in Porto.

Emergencies

For police, fire and ambulance services, dial ☎112.

Public holidays

In addition to Christmas (Dec 24–25) and New Year's Day (Jan 1), public holidays include Good Friday (March/April); April 25 (Liberty Day); May 1 (Labour Day); June 10 (Portugal/Camões Day); June 24 (São João, Porto only); August 15 (Feast of the Assumption); 5 October (Republic Day); 1 November (All Saints' Day); December 1 (Independence Day); December 8 (Immaculate Conception).

Left luggage

There are coin-operated lockers at the Campanhã and São Bento train stations.

LGBTQ+ travellers

For listings, support and news, visit ⊚ portugalgay.pt (in Portuguese only).

Libraries

The Biblioteca Municipal Almeida Garrett is at Palácio de Cristal, Rua Dom Manuel II; Biblioteca Municipal do Porto is on Rua Dom João VI.

Lost property

The Tourism Police is at Rua Clube dos Fenianos 11 (☎ 222 081 833).

Money

Portugal uses the euro (€). Banks open Monday to Friday 8.30am–3pm. Most branches have automatic exchange machines for various currencies.

Opening hours

Most shops open Monday to Saturday 9am–7pm; smaller shops close for lunch (around 1–3pm) and also on Saturday afternoons; shopping centres are usually open daily until 10pm.

Most museums and monuments open Tuesday to Sunday 10am–6pm.

Post offices

Post offices (correios) are usually open Monday to Friday 8.30am–6pm. The main post office is on Praça General Humberto Delgado, by the town hall. Stamps (selos) are sold anywhere with the sign "Correio de Portugal – Selos".

Price codes

Accommodation (see box, page 115) and eating out listings (see box, below) throughout the Guide have been categorized according to a price code.

Smoking

Smoking is prohibited in most restaurants and cafés.

Sports

Porto have punched above their weight in European football for years. They have won the Portuguese league nearly thirty times, though their crowning glory was the European Cup win in 1987, and the Champions League win in 2004 (also won the 2003 UEFA Cup and the 2011 Europa League). You can

Eating out price codes

Throughout the Guide, eating out listings are categorized according to the following price ranges. Price categories reflect the cost of a two-course meal for one, without alcohol.

€	under €20
€€	€20–30
€€€	€30–45
€€€€	over €45

take a tour of Estádio do Dragão or buy match tickets (see page 124). You can also see top league action at the Estádio do Bessa, home to the city's second team, Boavista.

Tickets

Tickets for most shows (€15–50) can be bought from the FNAC books and music store, which also promotes gigs, events and talks. Porto's daily newspaper, the *Jornal de Notícias* is a useful source of information.

Time

Portuguese time is the same as GMT. Clocks go forward an hour in late March and back to GMT in late October.

Tipping

Service is often included in hotel and restaurant bills (usually ten percent); hotel porters and toilet attendants expect at least €1 for their help.

Toilets

There are very few public toilets, although most tourist sights have them (signed as *casa de banho*, *retrete*, *banheiro*, *lavabos* or "WC"). Gents are usually marked "H" (*homens*) or "C" (*cabalheiros*), and ladies "M" (*mulheres*) or "S" (*senhoras*).

Tourist information

The city's **Turismo Central** is at Rua Clube dos Fenianos 25 (daily: May–July & Sept–Oct 9am–8pm; Aug 9am–9pm; Nov–April 9am–7pm; ☎ 223 393 472), while the **Turismo Sé** is in Casa da Câmara (daily: May–Oct 9am–8pm; Nov–April 9am–7pm; ☎ 223 393 472). A **Tourism Information desk** at the airport offers local maps. Information points are on Praça da Liberdade (May–Oct daily 9.30am–6.30pm; Nov–April Mon–Fri 9.30am–5pm); in Campanhã train station (July & Aug only 9.30am–6.30pm) and on the

Tours and cruises

Porto's stock-in-trade is the **river cruise** along the Douro. Services leave daily from the jetty at Ribeira, or opposite in Vila Nova de Gaia: they are frequent in the summer and reduced between November and February. The cheapest is the fifty-minute bridges cruise (from €20), though there are also evening and dinner cruises, and full-day or weekend cruises, with prices ranging from €60 to €200. The longer cruises operate via the port wine town of Peso da Régua, halfway along the Douro, where you're either shuttled around a port wine lodge or go on a steam train. Other city tours include **open-top bus tours** such as the Hop-On-Hop-Off tour (ⓦcity-sightseeing.com) departing from Torre dos Clérigos; **tuk-tuk tours** (ⓦtuktourporto.com) leaving from Rua de São Filipe de Nery; free **walking tours** (ⓦportofreewalkingtour.wixsite.com/portofreewalkingtour/ fashion) departing from Praça de Gomes Teixeira near Livraria Lello; and Bluedragon City **bike tours** departing from Avenida Aliados and **segway tours** departing from Ribeira. The **Taste Porto Food Tour** (ⓦtasteporto.com) focuses on local gastronomy. **Porto Tours** at Rua Clube dos Fenianos 25 (ⓦportotours. com) can book river cruises, classic car tours and Vespa tours. **Cooltour Oporto** (Rua Júlio Dinis 728–3; ⓦcooltouroporto.com) offers package trips and personalized trips around Porto, and further afield for example in the Minho region.

Ribeira waterfront at Praça da Ribeira (April–Oct daily 10.30am–7pm).

Vila Nova de Gala has its own useful *turismo* on the waterfront at Av Diogo Leite 135 (April–Sept daily 10am–6pm; Oct–March Mon–Sat 10am–6pm; ☎ 223 758 288, ⓦ cm-gaia.pt), which is geared almost exclusively to pointing you towards the port wine lodges.

There are also tourist offices at the day-trip destinations of **Vila do Conde** at Rua 25 de Abril 103 (June to mid-Sept Mon–Fri 9am–7pm, Sat & Sun 9.30am–1pm & 2.30–6pm; mid-Sept to May Mon–Fri 9.30am–12.30pm & 2–6pm; ☎ 252 248 473, ⓦ cm-viladoconde.pt); and **Amarante** at the Information Turismo, Largo Conselheiro António Candido (daily: June–Sept 9.30am–7pm; Oct–May 9.30am–12.30pm & 2–6pm; ☎ 255 420 246, ⓦ cm-amarante.pt/turismo).

There are lots of **online information resources**, including the main tourist office website ⓦ visitporto.travel which has detailed information in English on everything from the main sites to events, while there's more information about Porto and the north of Portugal on ⓦ visitportoandnorth.travel. For a different view of the city, check out ⓦ oportocool.wordpress.com, a blog of the city's fashionable hotspots (blog is in Portuguese).

Festivals and events

You can check exact festival and event dates on Visit Portugal's tourism website ⓦ visitportugal.com/en. One-off and less mainstream events can be found on ⓦ infoporto.pt, which has information in both Portuguese and English. The website ⓦ viralagenda.com/pt/porto is another good resource but is only in Portuguese.

Fantasporto

February–March
ⓦ fantasporto.com

The respected international fantasy, sci-fi and thriller film festival, has been a fixture in the city since 1980. The festival runs over ten days and takes place at the Rivoli Theatre, at Rua do Bonjardim 143.

Queima das Fitas do Porto

May

The city's "burning of the ribbons" represents the big end-of-year festival for Porto's students (the ribbons representing the various faculties). There are concerts and fado performances hosted throughout the city, as well as a procession in the Parque da Cidade.

São João

June

Porto lets its hair down during the exuberant celebration that is the Festa de São João, St John's Eve (the night of June 23–24), in honour of John the Baptist, patron saint of the city. Be warned, for one night only it is considered fair game to bash total strangers over the head, traditionally with leeks, though now these have been replaced by even more irritating squeaky plastic hammers. There are free concerts throughout the night and a massive firework display at midnight over the river at Praça da Ribeira. The following morning there's a traditional Rabelo boat regatta on the Douro.

Festas da Cidade

June

The Festa de São João party is the highlight of the wider city festival, the Festas da Cidade, that runs throughout the whole month of June and celebrates the start of the summer season with a mix of music concerts, dances, vintage car rallies, regattas, sardine grills and other riotous entertainments – like the competitive cascata displays (dolls depicting Santo António, São João and São Pedro, complete with miniature houses, trains and cars).

Festa da Cerveja

June
The annual Festa da Cerveja (Beer Fest) runs for five days in the Jardim do Palácio de Cristal, with around two hundred national and international craft beers together with street-food stalls and live music.

Nos Primavera Sound

June Ⓦ nosprimaverasound.com
A big music festival held in the Parque da Cidade. Past acts have included Jarvis Cocker, Lizzo, Interpol, and James Blake.

Fazer a Festa International Theatre Festival

July Ⓦ teatroartimagem.org
This major international theatre festival has thirty professional theatre companies and around sixty theatrical performances held in squares, gardens and cultural spaces around the city, aimed particularly at getting young people into theatre.

LGBTQ Porto Pride

July
First held in 2001 and growing in size each year, the LGBTQ Porto Pride march and celebration takes place in the first or second week of July, departing from Praça da República.

The Porto Wine Fest

July
Taking place along the river front at Vila Nova de Gaia, the Porto Wine Fest features wine tastings, food stalls showcasing recipes by leading chefs and events laid on by the major port-wine lodges.

Noites Ritual

September
The Noites Ritual is an exclusively Portuguese music festival with performances at the Rota Mota Pavilion in the Jardim do Palácio de Cristal. Free entry.

Porto Jazz Festival

September Ⓦ portajazz.com
Porto's jazz festival is held during the month of September in the Jardim do Palácio de Cristal, with local and international performers.

Christmas

December
The Christmas period in Porto sees the historic centre decked out in glittering Christmas lights. The main celebration is Midnight Mass on 24 December followed by a huge meal of *bacalhau*. Some cafés and restaurants are open on 25 December.

Corrida de São Silvestre and New Year

December
A running race departing from Av dos Aliados to mark the end of the year. New Year is welcomed with a firework display over the river, after which you can find traditional *bolo rei* cakes in cafés and shops.

Chronology

4th century AD Romans form a port on the north bank of the Douro and call it Portus Cale.

711–868 Moorish occupation, which ends when a Christian warlord, Count Vimara Peres, takes control of the district between the Minho and the Douro, which is now called Condado de Portucale.

1095 Henri of Burgundy is granted the land around Portucale. His son, Afonso Henriques, becomes king of a newly independent country named Portugal.

1111 Bishop Hugo begins work on the city's cathedral and walls as the city grows around the Ribeira.

12th century The beginning of port-wine production. Grapes are taken to the lodges on the humid south side of the river in Vila Nova de Gaia where conditions are best, and Porto begins to export port.

1387 After staying in the church of São Francisco, Dom João I marries Philippa of Lancaster in Porto to cement the alliance between England and Portugal. The city begins to grow.

1394 The son of Philippa of Lancaster and João I, Henry the Navigator, is born in Porto. He becomes the driving force behind Portugal's explorations of the oceans. Sturdy city walls are built to protect Porto from attack.

15th–17th century Porto becomes one of the largest shipbuilding centres in the country as Portugal's navigators expand the country's maritime empire, which extends from Brazil in the west to Macau in the east.

1415 Porto residents donate meat to sailors heading off to conquer Ceuta in Africa, keeping only tripe to feed themselves. From this time on, Porto residents are known as *tripeiros*, and it is still a local speciality.

16th century AD Under Dom Manuel I, the riverside city expands outwards, with the creation of streets such as Rua das Flores and churches such as the Convento de Santa Clara and Mosteiro de São Bento da Vitoria.

1703 The Methuen Treaty between Portugal and England stimulates trade with Britain and guarantees sales of port at a time when standard wines were hard to come by in England because of war with the French.

1717 The first English factory is set up in Porto as the port industry becomes run largely by the British.

1757 The Marquês de Pombal creates the Demarcated Region of the Alto Douro to control the quality of wine production.

17th–18th century AD Public works projects see the building of the Torre de Clérigos. The millinery industry grows up as the city becomes more industrialized, with textiles, iron-mongery and linen the other mainstays. Most of the city walls are demolished to make way for development.

1809 Napoleon occupies Porto. Many residents die when fleeing across a flimsy pontoon bridge over the Douro. Napoleon is soon driven from city, with the help of the British who, under Wellington, cross the Douro on port boats to chase out the French.

1832–1834 Liberal Porto residents resist an 18-month siege by the antiliberal constitution troops loyal to Dom Miguel during the Portuguese civil war, establishing the Porto residents' reputation for being tough.

19th century Industrialization continues, with many ceramics factories opening. The century also sees the building of the Mercado do Bolhão, the laying out of city parks, the arrival of gas street lighting and water supplies.

1843 The first permanent bridge is built over the Douro, the Ponte Pênsil, which is soon replaced in 1886 by the Ponte de Dom Luís I, built by Teophile Seyrig, a partner of Eiffel.

1877 The Ponte Maria Pia opens for Porto's railway, built by Gustave Eiffel. It is replaced by the Ponte de São João in 1991.

1890 Economic recession leads to a republican revolt in Porto which eventually leads to the creation of the Portuguese Republic in 1910.

1919 A counter-revolution in Porto to reestablish the monarchy is squashed.

1933 The Instituto dos Vinhos do Douro e do Porto is set up to regulate the port wine trade.

1945 Porto's airport opens 11km north west of the centre.

1950s Sales of port slump after World War II. Many independent port companies are bought out by international drinks chains.

1970s Taylors launch Late Bottled Vintage Port, a quality port which was more affordable than vintage.

1996 Porto is named a UNESCO World Heritage Site.

2001 Porto is named European Capital of Culture.

2002 The first metro line opens in Porto. It extends to the airport in 2006.

2004 The Estádio do Dragão is built to host the football European Championships, in the same year as José Mourinho's FC Porto win the European Champions League.

2009 Ryanair become the first low-cost airline to fly to Porto. Others soon follow suit.

2015 A new cruise terminal opens at Leixões, north of the city.

2018 Porto city council introduces a €2 city tax for all tourists.

2019 Portugal wins the UEFA Nations League at Estádio do Dragão, Porto.

2022 Costa's Socialist Party wins a rare majority government in elections.

2023 Work underway on two new metro lines: Line G (Pink Line), which will connect Casa da Música to São Bento through Cordoaria, and Ruby Line H, which will run between Casa da Música and Santo Ovídio in Vila Nova de Gaia (the project will include a new bridge over the Douro).

Language

English is widely spoken in most of Porto's hotels and tourist restaurants, but you will find a few words of Portuguese extremely useful. Written

Portuguese is similar to Spanish, though pronunciation is very different. Vowels are often nasal or ignored altogether. The consonants, at least, are consistent:

Consonants

c is soft before e and i, hard otherwise unless it has a cedilla – *açúcar* (sugar) is pronounced "assookar".

ch is somewhat softer than in English; *chá* (tea) sounds like Shah.

j is like the "s" in pleasure, as is g except when it comes before a "hard" vowel (a, o and u).

lh sounds like "lyuh".

q is always pronounced as a "k".

s before a consonant or at the end of a word becomes "sh", otherwise it's as in English – *caracóis* (snails) is pronounced "Karakoish".

x is also pronounced "sh"– Baixa is pronounced "Baisha".

Vowels

e/é e at the end of a word is silent unless it has an accent, so that *carne* (meat) is pronounced "karn", while *café* is "caf-ay".

ã or õ the tilde renders the pronunciation much like the French -an and -on endings, only more nasal.

ão this sounds something like a strangled "Ow!" cut off in midstream (as in *pão*, bread – *são*, saint – *limão*, lemon).

ei this sounds like "ay" (as in *feito* – finished).

ou this sounds like "oh" (as in *roupa* – clothes).

Words and phrases

Basics

yes sim
no não
hello olá
good morning bom dia
good afternoon/night boa tarde/noite
goodbye adeus
see you later até logo
today hoje
tomorrow amanhã
please por favor/se faz favor
everything all right? tudo bem?
it's all right/OK está bem
thank you (male/female speaker) obrigado/a
where onde
what que
when quando
why porquê

how como
how much quanto
I don't know não sei
do you know...? sabe...?
could you...? pode...?
is there...? there is há...? (silent "h")
do you have...? tem...? (pron. "taying")
I'd like... queria...
sorry desculpe
excuse me com licença
do you speak English? fala Inglês?
I don't understand não compreendo
this este/a
that esse/a
now agora
later mais tarde
more mais
less menos
big grande
little pequeno
open aberto
closed fechado
women senhoras
men homens
toilet/bathroom lavabo/quarto de banho

Getting around

left esquerda
right direita
straight ahead sempre em frente
here aqui
there ali
near perto
far longe
Where is... Onde é...
  the bus station? a estação de camionetas?
  the bus stop for... a paragem de autocarro para...
Where does the bus to...leave from? Donde parte o autocarro para...?
What time does it leave? (arrive at...?) A que horas parte (chega a...?) ?
Stop here please Pare aqui por favor
ticket (to) bilhete (para)
return trip ida e volta

Common signs

open aberto
closed fechado

entrance entrada
exit saída
pull puxe
push empurre
lift elevador
pay in advance pré-pagamento
danger/ous perigo/perigoso
no parking proibido estacionar
(road) works obras

Accommodation

I'd like a room Queria um quarto
It's for one night (week) É para uma noite (semana)
It's for one person (two people) É para uma pessoa (duas pessoas)
How much is it? Quanto custa?
May I see/ look? Posso ver?
Is there a cheaper room? Há um quarto mais barato?
with a shower com duche

Shopping

How much is it? Quanto é?
bank; change banco; câmbio
post office correios
(two) stamps (dois) selos
What's this called in Portuguese? Como se diz isto em Português?
What's that? O que é isso?
sale saldo
sold out esgotado

Days of the week

Sunday Domingo
Monday Segunda-feira
Tuesday Terça feira
Wednesday Quarta-feira
Thursday Quinta-feira
Friday Sexta-feira
Saturday Sábado

Months

January Janeiro
February Fevereiro
March Março
April Abril
May Maio
June Junho
July Julho

August Agosto
September Setembro
October Outubro
November Novembro
December Dezembro

Useful words

glazed, painted tile azulejo
quay cais
chapel capela
house casa
shopping centre centro commercial
station estação
street/road estrada/rua
fair or market feira
church igreja
garden jardim
viewpoint/belvedere miradouro
square praça/largo

Numbers

1 um/uma
2 dois/duas
3 três
4 quatro
5 cinco
6 seis
7 sete
8 oito
9 nove
10 dez
11 onze
12 doze
13 treze
14 catorze
15 quinze
16 dezasseis
17 dezassete
18 dezoito
19 dezanove
20 vinte
21 vinte e um
30 trinta
40 quarenta
50 cinquenta
60 sessenta
70 setenta
80 oitenta
90 noventa
100 cem

101 cento e um
200 duzentos
500 quinhentos
1000 mil

Food and drink

Basics

assado roasted
colher spoon
conta bill
copo glass
cozido boiled
ementa menu
estrelado/frito fried
faca knife
garfo fork
garrafa bottle
grelhado grilled
mexido scrambled

Menu terms

almoço lunch
ementa turística set menu
entradas starters
especialidades speciality
jantar dinner
lista de vinhos wine list
pequeno almoço breakfast
petiscos tapas-like snacks
prato do dia dish of the day
sobremesa dessert

Soups, salad and staples

açúcar sugar
arroz rice
azeitonas olives
batatas fritas chips/french fries
caldo verde cabbage soup
fruta fruit
legumes vegetables
manteiga butter
massa pasta
molho (de tomate/piri-piri) tomato/chilli
sauce)
omeleta omelette
ovos eggs
pão bread
pimenta pepper
piri-piri chilli sauce

queijo cheese
sal salt
salada salad
sopa de legumes vegetable soup
sopa de marisco shellfish soup
sopa de peixe fish soup

Fish and shellfish

atum tuna
camarões shrimp
carapau mackerel
cherne stone bass
dourada bream
espada scabbard fish
espadarte swordfish
gambas prawns
lagosta lobster
lulas (grelhadas) squid (grilled)
mexilhões mussels
pescada hake
polvo octopus
robalo sea bass
salmão salmon
salmonete red mullet
santola spider crab
sapateira crab
sardinhas sardines
tamboril monkfish
truta trout
viera scallop

Meat

alheira chicken sausage
borrego lamb
chanfana lamb or goat casserole
chouriço spicy sausage
coelho rabbit
cordeiro lamb
dobrada/tripa tripe
espetada mista mixed meat kebab
febras pork steaks
fiambre ham
fígado liver
frango na brasa chicken grilled over hot
coals
frango no churrasco barbecued chicken
leitão roast suckling pig
pato duck
perdiz partridge
perú turkey

picanha strips of beef in garlic sauce
presunto smoked ham
rim kidney
rodizio barbecued meats
rojões cubed pork cooked in blood with potatoes
vitela veal

Portuguese specialities

açorda bread-based stew (often seafood)
arroz de marisco seafood rice
bife à portuguesa thin beef steak with a fried egg on top
bacalhau à brás salted cod with egg and potatoes
bacalhau na brasa salted cod roasted with potatoes
bacalhau à Gomes de Sá salted cod baked with potatoes, egg and olives
caldeirada fish stew
cataplana fish, shellfish or meat stewed in a circular metal dish
cozido à portuguesa boiled casserole of meat and beans, served with rice and vegetables
feijoada bean stew with meat and vegetables
filletes de pescada hake fillets in a light batter
francesinha toasted meat sandwich with cheese sauce

migas meat or fish in a bready garlic sauce
pataniscas *bacalhau* patties, salted cod cakes
porco à alentejana pork cooked with clams
tripas à modo do Porto tripe and bean stew

Snacks and desserts

arroz doce rice pudding
bifana steak sandwich
bolo cake
gelado ice cream
pastéis de bacalhau salted cod and potato cakes
pastel de nata custard tart
prego steak sandwich
pudim crème caramel
tosta toasted sandwich

Drinks

água (sem/com gás) mineral water (without/with gas)
café coffee
cerveja beer
chá tea
fresca/natural chilled/room temperature
sem/com leite without/with milk
sem/com açúcar without/with sugar
sumo de laranja/maçã orange/apple juice
um copo/uma garrafa de/da... a glass/bottle of...
vinho branco/tinto white/red wine

SMALL PRINT

Publishing information
Second edition 2024

Distribution
UK, Ireland and Europe
Apa Publications (UK) Ltd; sales@roughguides.com
United States and Canada
Ingram Publisher Services; ips@ingramcontent.com
Australia and New Zealand
Booktopia; retailer@booktopia.com.au
Worldwide
Apa Publications (UK) Ltd; sales@roughguides.com

Special Sales, Content Licensing and CoPublishing
Rough Guides can be purchased in bulk quantities at discounted prices. We can create special editions, personalised jackets and corporate imprints tailored to your needs. sales@roughguides.com.

roughguides.com

Printed in Czech Republic

This book was produced using **Typefi** automated publishing software.

A catalogue record for this book is available from the British Library
The publishers and authors have done their best to ensure the accuracy and currency of all the information in **Pocket Rough Guide Porto**, however, they can accept no responsibility for any loss, injury, or inconvenience sustained by any traveller as a result of information or advice contained in the guide.

Rough Guide credits
Editor: Joanna Reeves
Cartography: Carte
Picture Editor: Tom Smyth
Layout: Pradeep Thapliyal
Original design: Richard Czapnik
Head of DTP and Pre-Press: Rebeka Davies
Head of Publishing: Sarah Clark

About the author

Joanna Reeves is a Sussex-based travel writer who has updated several guidebooks, including the *Rough Guide to England*, *Pocket Rough Guide Reykjavík* and *Rough Guide Mini Bologna*. She is also the editor of the brand-new *Rough Guide to Slow Travel in Europe*.

Help us update

We've gone to a lot of effort to ensure that this edition of the **Pocket Rough Guide Porto** is accurate and up-to-date. However, things change – places get "discovered", opening hours are notoriously fickle, restaurants and rooms raise prices or lower standards. If you feel we've got it wrong or left something out, we'd like to know, and if you can remember the address, the price, the hours, the phone number, so much the better.

Please send your comments with the subject line "**Pocket Rough Guide Porto Update**" to mail@uk.roughguides.com. We'll credit all contributions and send a copy of the next edition (or any other Rough Guide if you prefer) for the very best emails.

Photo Credits

(Key: T-top; C-centre; B-bottom; L-left; R-right)

Alamy 20C, 55, 70, 80
daTerra 88
Dreamstime 14T, 18C, 19T, 20B, 22B, 77, 86, 101
Gail Edwin Aguiar 89
Gonçalo/The Wine Box 35
Guindalense futebal clube 46
iStock 4, 11T, 11B, 12/13T, 12B, 26, 30, 49, 51, 57, 60, 63, 76, 91, 92, 103, 107, 120/121
Largo do Paço 111
Luc Hermans 104
Matthew Hancock/Porto Convention & Visitors Bureau 98
Miguel Marques/3 + Arte 69
Pedro Costa/Amarante Tourism 110
Pedro Mendes/O Comercial 33

Plano B 58
Porto Convention & Visitors Bureau 56, 66, 72
Porto Cruz 71
Renato Ribeiro/Tapas & Music Bar 12/13B
scar-id store 79
Shutterstock 1, 2T, 2BL, 2C, 2BR, 5, 6, 10, 13C, 15T, 15B, 16T, 16B, 17T, 17B, 18T, 18B, 19C, 19B, 21T, 21C, 21B, 22T, 22C, 23T, 23C, 23B, 24/25, 34, 36, 40, 42, 45, 52, 65, 75, 81, 83, 94, 96, 109, 112/113
Tavi 97
Tendinha dos Clérigos 59
Vila do Conde Municipal Arquive 105
World of Wine Museum 14B

Cover Capela das Almas **Shutterstock**

Index

NOTES